THE SECRET HISTORY

THE SECRET HISTORY

Cosmos, History, Post-Mortem Transformation Mysteries,
and the Dark Spiritual Ecology of Witchcraft

By
Robin Artisson

Illustrations By
Stephanie Houser

ISBN-13:
978-1535006613
ISBN-10:
1535006617

BLACK MALKIN PRESS
Algonac, MI

www.robinartisson.com

For the Gude People Seen and Unseen

CONTAINED HEREIN

Introduction: Telling the Story of the World

"The Secret History" is about how everything came to be, and what that means for us right now. Obviously, there have been many attempts to tell the story of the world and a story of destiny for human beings, but most of those attempts suffer from a narrowness of perspective born in various religious and civilized assumptions about the world. Where those stories take us- in spirit, and in everyday, tangible outcomes- cannot rise above the limited power of their origins.

So I have sought a different set of starting points, a different realm of provenance, a different family of origin-powers for my own attempt at telling the story. I have looked to myth and folklore to identify the faces and forms of older powers, dimly remembered by human beings and sometimes invisible. These powers are real; they are our Ancestors, and they play a crucial role in the true story of us, however little we remember them. They are real, living powers who have not gone anywhere- we are the ones who have surely "gone somewhere" far from them in our understandings and in our perceptions.

We didn't mean for this to happen. None of us chose to be born where we were born, and to come under the influence of the powers of forgetting quite like we all have, but it happened. Stories that shouldn't make sense make perfect sense to us because they satisfy assumptions we hold but never question. We don't often realize that we *have* assumptions, and so they seem to be simple and natural parts of our own beings.

This is a book that posits more than just a unique view of cosmology based on ancient concepts and powers; this is a book that also reveals the essence of real *mysteries*. It's hard to talk about mysteries in the modern day, because the last true mystery schools vanished a long time ago; their work only continued in the most obscure forms, folk-tales and fire-side poetry. These forms allow the transformative force of mystery-ideas and mystery-stories to persist in a subtle way, but they no longer appear as accessible institutions that welcome any initiate who might be prepared beforehand.

They appear as dark bodies of water, full of power below the surface but whose presence is only enjoyed in the way we enjoy moonlight reflecting peacefully on the surface of a pond. Just being near enough to the pond makes you feel some measure of serenity, but you don't really have the words to explain why. If you were to dive into the dark water you'd find yourself in a very powerful place indeed, but few people ever do.

No one really has ears to hear what mystery-understandings have to say about the world anymore, because they are so strange and out of step with the structure of the modern world that they appear (to most) as alien, evil, dangerous, primitive and scorn-worthy, or nonsensical. And that's assuming that many people get to see them or hear of them at all, which most don't.

Mysteries are largely about correcting, repairing, and healing the human experience, as it has turned sour or become isolated from wisdom and wholeness. They came in the cultural dress of real civilizations, long ago, but concealed the experience- the direct experience- of what most of those cultures could not admit to, could not say openly. They were secret because their perspectives were contrary to the common knowledge and standard wisdom so prominent in their times.

In another sense, mystery religions and cults had to be secret if they wanted to survive. They were forced to conduct their business- and mediate their realizations- in ways that didn't too greatly disrupt the workings of the "outer culture." Because what they all offered, what they all had to say, was not for common consumption.

To meet the Gods- the sacred forces worshiped by a people face-to-face- was not for everyone. To regain intimate communication with the dead, to see and experience the afterlife-condition that awaited all in death, to know one's place, to know how all the world came to be and whence came the wretched conditions that now proliferated: that person would have knowledge best reserved for the dead, and the Gods themselves.

No one with that kind of knowledge will submit to slavery. They will not submit to manipulation, and they will not be carried away by the shallow sentiments that rule the hearts of most. For an individual man or woman, that was a precious gift, and if they had the wits to remain judiciously silent, it was the most precious of things. But society as a whole could not have such gifts; such a society would never survive. The force of truth appears as a grim destroyer when a society is carefully based on complex systems of untruth.

That such societies should exist *at all* is precisely why mysteries came to be. It was this disease of interaction, this degeneracy of the mortal power to live fairly and freely that made a pained call into the Deep, and the Deep *responded*. It wasn't just mortal men and women who preserved long-forgotten truths and found ways to communicate them in private to people attending to the mysteries; nothing so banal ever occurred.

Such is the nature of the great powers that appeared to bend and warp human social systems into cobwebs of deceit, that mortal men and women could never have managed to hold on to the lost truths of many ages past, not even in distorted, dimly remembered forms. Mortals cannot compete, alone and unaided, with the forces that weave slavery and unwisdom.

It was the Company of the Unseen World, "*Them*" who live outside of the cobwebs of mortal deceit, who remembered and who took the initiative to communicate in deep mystical intimacy these lost truths to human beings. It was those blessed human beings, working in conjunction with Great Spiritual Beings, who established mystery schools and cults.

The mysteries are not machinations of mortality; they are intrusions of the spiritual potencies of the Netherworld into human affairs. They are gifts of the Gods. They are the "evidence of things Unseen"- and not the mystery-initiations and practices themselves, but what experiences they lead to. They lead to certainty about the strangest and most sacred forces that we have lost our ability to easily experience. They lead, eventually, to the "Wordless

Understanding" that frees us. This book takes the important concept of the *Indweller*, and breathes further life into it. In my book "Letters from the Devil's Forest" I first introduced the idea of the Indweller for use in understanding and speaking about the spiritual powers dealt with by witches and sorcerers, within the webwork of dark spiritual ecology that I consider to be native and natural to witchcraft and sorcery.

What follows is an excerpt from that book describing what Indwellers are and how they exist. The explanations given are from Daniel Merkur's excellent book *Powers Which We Do Not Know*, the superb work that first helped me to comprehend the full reality of the Indwellers and to communicate it. I include it here for your ease of understanding what I will be discussing in greater detail in this work.

"The Indweller is a power immanent inside of a particular phenomenon. By indwelling the phenomenon, the phenomenon is rendered "real" or rendered potent, powerful, and able to be interacted with by others- it becomes a vibrant presence in the intersubjective world. Merkur quotes Nicholas Gubser's description of the Indwellers in this way:

"*An inua (indweller) is not the personality or even a characteristic of an object or phenomenon, although an inua itself may have a personality. The spirit (or indweller) of an object or phenomenon may be thought of, in the case of so-called "inanimate" objects, as the essential existing force of that object. Without an indweller or spirit, an object might still occupy space, and have weight, but it would have no meaning, it would have no real existence. When an object is invested or inhabited by an indweller, it is a part of nature of which we are aware."*

The Indweller, as Merkur then points out, is the differential factor that transforms "matter", abstractly considered, into a discrete and living sensual phenomenon.

Merkur brings to bear Birket-Smith's superb statement regarding who the Indwellers are, precisely; he says "*Every object, every rock, every phenomenon- are living. Everything has a living indweller- the indwellers are manifestations of the vitality of nature herself.*"

 The ethnographer Rasmussen had little ability to comprehend indwellers among the Inuit as anything other than "gods", but he made a useful mention of them in his own recordings wherein he wrote

"The idea of God, or group of gods, to be worshiped, is altogether alien to the Inuit mind. They know only powers or personifications of natural forces acting upon human life in various ways and affecting all that lives through fair and foul weather, disease and perils of all kinds. These powers are not evil in themselves, they do not wreak harm of evil intent, but they are nevertheless dangerous owing to their unmerciful severity where men fail to live in accordance with the wise rules of life decreed by their forefathers."

Of course, Rasmussen, a Christian, fell easily into the popular notion (in his time) that Heathen peoples of all types and from every age and place were merely worshiping "personifications" of natural phenomenon. But Indwellers are not mere personifications of anything. They are persons, indwelling various natural phenomena, and have always been so. And conscious human interaction with them, all over the world, was ongoing (and remains ongoing in some places) until the modern age when human beings in the West and in other places fell away from the intricate network of maintained relationships with them that characterized nearly all of our history as people. It is beyond a doubt that the mightiest Indwellers- upon whom man relies so much for things as essential as his breath or his food- were and are the beings that stand behind our Western notions of "God" and "Gods" from earlier times.

But the Indwellers are, straightly stated, spirits. And potent, ancient spirits, powerful entities of this universal type- themselves born of the sheer vitality of Nature herself ("Nature" here referring to the entire network of fateful forces that bring everything into being)- can be and absolutely were worshiped as Gods or Goddesses all over the world in the past, and still today. The term "god" is a matter of cultural aesthetic and language.

Merkur goes behind Rasmussen and says what needed to be said in the shortest, most perfect manner: *"Indwellers can be termed personifications of natural forces only from a Western point of view. To Inuit thought, **indwellers are the powers that constitute Nature.**"*

Merkur completes his superb analysis of the concept of "in-dweller" by stating

"Outside the human mind, indwellers are specific in location to the phenomenon whose forms they impart. Like the phenomenon, they may variously be unchanging, mutable, or destructible. In principle, all phenomenon is structured by indwellers. In practice, only a few major indwellers, whose changes have important consequences for Inuit well-being, have prominence within Inuit religion: The Indweller in the Wind, The Indweller in the Earth... the Sea Mother, the Moon Man, and locally, the indwellers in coves, capes, etc. Indwellers are completely autonomous and disinterested in people. Inuit can hurt themselves by abusing indwellers, or derive benefits by being in accord with them. In both cases, indwellers are what they are, with neither positive nor negative ambitions towards human beings. Because the Wind Indweller has a stern personality, Arctic weather is often fierce. In summer, his temper is better. Because the Sea Mother is jealous and vindictive, the sea is dangerous and miserly in its provision of game. Because the Moon Man has a benevolent disposition, the moon casts a benign light during the long winter nights. Neither the basic temperaments of the Indwellers, nor the consequent characteristics of the phenomenon in which they indwell are determined by human activity. However, because indwellers are anthropopsychic, they are not beyond the reach of social intercourse."

Merkur's statement "indwellers are specific in location to the phenomenon whose forms they impart" reveals something immediately: two specific Indwellers (the masculine-depicted being who Indwells the wind, the sky, and the weather, and the feminine-depicted being who Indwells the Earth itself) are *universal Indwellers* who can be found at every moment,

8

anywhere you could be on earth. Even if you were on a boat in the middle of an ocean, upon which your sails would still encounter the Wind Indweller, if you dove down far enough, the Earth Indweller's body- the Earth itself- would still be present."

* * *

I am going to construct a very simple, very organic cosmology of types, centered around the Wind or World Indweller and the Earth Indweller. I believe that this cosmological pat- tern that I will establish will be easy to see shining forth from inside most perennial patterns of myth and folklore concerning world-creation and the "nature of nature." I am attempting to create something like a proto-myth, but I won't be telling a formal story; I will be discussing these powers that exist along with ideas about how they might have come to exist, and how they interacted to help us exist.

But I will also be discussing something that may appear to be a "dark turn" sideways from that: I will be discussing the fall of the human world, directly put. I don't mean a "fall" that is consequent to an invasion of human moral depravity, as we find in mainstream monotheistic religions. I mean the strange situations and circumstances that overcame human beings at the dawn of civilization, which made us turn away from older forms of connection and experience with the greater community of life.

The consequences of this "turning away" weren't just terrible on us; they were terrible on the entities that we once encountered as the persons of animals, plants, trees, mountains, and waters, too. They were terrible for our communication with those who had journeyed into and beyond death but who still continued to exist, though now unseen, feared, or forgotten.

This turning away- this great disease of the spirit that reflects into our every action, thought, feeling, and activity- is the true cause of all the miseries and the deep sense of existential alienation and isolation that we have suffered individually and collectively ever since. This might be considered one of the mystery-realizations that civilizations cannot tolerate at too public a level within their midst.

The mystery-truth is too simple and too terrible to bear: the basic assumptions we have about how we live and how we should live, and what is good and what is evil, may be so flawed or out of step with reality that *any* attempt to normalize them and live under their logic results in a soul-deep pain, and a slow decay or decline for the body, the soul, and the collective society all around over a long enough of a time.

I am not only going to talk about this definitive quandary of the human species (and which troubles far more than just human beings) but also *two specific means,* both born in Otherworldly activity, that came at some point in the distant past to "meet us halfway" and help us find our way homeward to freedom from pain and isolation. I admit that eschatology is not something I ever imagined I'd be writing a lot about, but as my own life progresses, and as I become more world-aware, I realize the need for it, not just for me but for many. Part of why this book came to be was to satisfy just that awareness, and what I felt it required of me.

I wanted, for years, to have a story I could use to see my world through; a story that didn't bear blatant and obvious flaws or ancient agendas born in antique social politics, antique civilized economics, antique patriarchy, nor any of these clearly human interpolations into what should be a story about the sacred powers of our world.

I wanted a story that was as clean and clear as the streams I found in forests far away from the beaten trails. I wanted a way to comprehend the many parts of my experience- a natural mosaic to put them in- that rendered to them what I felt was *due respect and reverence*, and made me feel like I had satisfied my duty to the beauty and simplicity and spiritual fitness of life itself.

My story would need some challenging elements too, but again, *natural ones*, for Nature is a field not just of harmonizing powers, but of contending ones as well, and Her powers can be very strange and frightening at times. But the story needed to be a story about the world, *from* the world, as free from obvious politics and unwise human agendas as possible.

My story, I thought, should resonate with the best wisdom of the best folk-tales: the ones I knew contained real relics of wisdom within them, but the kinds of relics with secret messages that I could feel and sense, but never unravel completely. The story could not offend the most basic pylons of everyday experience, nor the natural reason in me; but I was comfortable with surreal elements that might defy the neatness of the tale, for the world is never really that neat.

That story finally emerged. With it came some very potent ideas and perspectives on not just where things came from and what they are now, but where I might be going when my future path finally runs into the shadowy obscurity beyond the boundaries that my mortal eyes can see or my mortal mind can conceive of.

With this work, I turn that story over to you in the spirit of helping you to re-story your world in such ways, if it pleases you to do so. I also turn over these mystery-perspectives that might help you to forge relationships with the Unseen that can change how you live in this world, how you die, and what happens after that, too.

May the Gude Powers extend their helpful hands.

Robin Artisson
Summer Solstice 2016

PART ONE

THE SECRET HISTORY

I: The Wordless Understanding

The Provenance term "*The Wordless Understanding*" is called so for several reasons. Titles for certain sorcerous or mystical paths like "The Nameless Way" are trying to express several things, but foremost among them is the idea that not every power or person we might encounter is going to be easy to name, or perhaps not even possible to name. The same is true with certain experiences. The final *understanding experience* that renders a person somehow at lasting peace with the world and all things, including themselves, defies easy naming.

I believe in this ultimate "peak understanding experience." I accord to it the position of a central goal of my whole personal philosophical approach, but I want to sound a note of caution about allowing anything to become too linear or "goal oriented" in the ordinary way that people often grasp such things. Even with the true fulfillment of our understanding of ourselves and the world or cosmos present, I don't think that we'll discover that we've reached the end of a contest or a game of some sort that was being played all along. I don't think we exist because the cosmos intends us to reach a "finish line" of types, or because we're being tested. Life's deepest point was never to overcome a confusion of some sort.

I think we are all simply enduring the many vicissitudes of life as best we can, in a natural, dynamic space of spontaneous life-emergence that we'll call "the world." The sorts of allies we can make to help endure and overcome those vicissitudes are one of the most important factors of any life, from my view.

Even with the benefit of some ultimate understanding, I think *life goes on*, as they say, and we continue to interact just as before, though perhaps wiser and with more ability to reduce the angst and sorrow that we might have felt as less wise beings previously. And the ultimate understanding might not be something obtained all at once; I'm very certain that it is not a one-time massive gain but a thing that grows slowly over time, and perhaps infinitely grows in a subtle way.

I do, however, think that we modern humans, ensconced within the boundaries of civilization and burdened with the many civilized assumptions that sharply divide us away from both the natural world and the Unseen world, are greatly hindered in the development of natural wisdom. I believe that certain earlier humans had an easier time grasping at natural wisdom, and certain earlier humans might not have had to make concerted efforts to grasp it at all.

I surely don't believe that the goal of wisdom (as I comprehend it) is a goal that has be *quite* this necessary in every age of the world previous to ours. Our present age has its unique struggles and its own unique existential drift.

The very idea that we can "structure the cosmos" along the lines of a mythos or a mythical system is suspect to me. The Wordless Understanding isn't just something you know without words, that leaves you whole and at peace. The Wordless Understanding is also, in a way, *the cosmos itself,* when it is allowed to be what it is, with no attempt made to make it fit into rigid story-structures.

I'm not saying that stories are bad. Stories are, in my way of seeing, all we really have. We have to use them to build better, wiser understandings and to interact with others better. And we do have quite the arsenal of stories produced by and told from all levels of culture and civilized history, as well as stories from pre-civilized history. We have our individual stories, too.

It so happens that, for the purposes of initiation, sometimes people have to be stripped of certain assumptions or hopes or dreams born in *certain kinds* of stories. The question in our present human life might not be a question of who's ultimately "right or wrong", but who has the best story with regard to the development of authentic wisdom.

II: The Occurrence

In my way of understanding there is a fundamental force, from a time much earlier than naming (though names could be created for it, and surely in the past have been.) This force is a root-power of the cosmos. It's an *occurrence*, a very potent and ongoing dynamism. This force, this occurrence, happens because the fateful structure of the cosmos *is the way it is*. Because the "Forces That Be" are the way they are, and because they relate the way they relate, this occurrence takes place and must *take* place. It is a consequence of the very skeletal structure of the world.

And this occurrence is, poetically expressed, very bright and full of motivation and power and creativity. It *makes* everything, if you want to look at it that way. It's not sitting around *choosing* to make everything; it's not a person as   we understand the term, choosing to do things. But it is ultimately why I'm sitting here writing this, and why you're reading it.

It is why you've been sexually aroused for another person before, or why you wrote a poem, or why you wander around looking at things with your eyes and thinking things about them, or why you want to survive and obtain things in this world. Everything that comes to be got to be that way because this great occurrence is very much a part of every place and time and combination of forces.

If there were Gods, or some race of very powerful and wise spirit-beings out there, the Gods would be Gods because of this occurrence, as readily as you're human, ultimately, because of it. The Gods would recognize this occurrence   in a very different way from how we ordinarily do. The Gods may have learned to perhaps "join" with it in a very different way, and maybe they enjoy it or learn from it or utilize it in different ways. Even Gods would think this basic quality of the world or the cosmos was holy or amazing. They might be mystified by it, themselves.

They might be (and in my view, certainly are) in *awe* of it, just like we humans can be when we become aware of it, and when we become aware of how intimately involved it is with everything, even down to the minute cellular activity of our bodies.

If a human person- or any person- could really be 100% aware of this occurrence, they'd be filled with a kind of infinite bliss or joy, as though the *basic power of life* is itself just a thing of happiness and an inexhaustible will to live.

So, if you step back a bit and look at the cosmos, you will see elemental powers existing, and many forces existing, all interacting, and *within* their interaction- all laced throughout them and driving them- is this occurrence. The occurrence, in conjunction with all those other things, makes life to appear in many forms. It makes humans, gods, spirits, squirrels, whales, oak trees, whatever exists and lives as a person or a particulate form of power that interacts with other forms of power.

This "boundless field of life force activity" that I'm calling (rather technically) "The Occurrence" was called *Zoë* by the ancient Greeks, and has been called other things by other cultures. In the language of symbols, which is ever deeper than human words, the ancients of Eastern Europe used the *Kolovrat* to symbolize the activity of this fecund, boundless life-generating force, which (as with nearly all people) was associated with the sun and solar activity and warmth. The *swastika* or *fylfot* in Northern and Western Europe (and other parts of the world, as far away as India and Central Asia and even the Americas) was also used to attempt to express its boundless dynamism.

These are all solar symbols, but I must mention that "The occurrence" is broader than solar-cult symbolism or beliefs. The sun is simply too strongly and obviously connected with the basic force of life itself for ancient humans to fail to center a lot of their intuitive expressions of deeper awe for the power of the occurrence around it, in iconography or myths or religious practices.

"The occurrence" is World-Dynamism, but also World-Fecundity, World-Impetus, and World-Urge; it includes more than just the sun's presence in the world, or the sun's interaction with other forces. The occurrence "made" life before there was a sun in the sky over our planet. There was a cosmos before the necessary combination of natural or cosmological forces brought our planet into its present form, and I believe that cosmos had many forms of life and entity within it before our planet came to be, and *still is* home to many orders of entity. I don't think many people would argue this point or possibility.

The occurrence is a consequence of the deepest, most known *and* most unknown pylons of the universe being arranged as they are. The matrix of cosmos is naturally a fecund, life-producing thing, and the universal activity of the occurrence will be conceptualized as a great light or life-force or power. It was even conceptualized (by some) as a divinity of some sort, though it seldom takes on too personal a form in most historical cultures. Some people in our very unwise modern day may persist in trying to over- personalize the occurrence, but I fastidiously avoid their thinking and their stories.

Because the occurrence is a life-generating inevitability of the cosmos-structure, in all its dynamism and perpetuity, the symbol of the *hex* (the hex-sign or the six-pointed star, three equal-length lines all meeting at their centers and splayed out so that the six arms so formed are all equidistant from one another) is the most appropriate symbol for it in my understanding.

The hex-sign would appear to be a natural structure (seen in every snowflake formed) that has always been associated with creation and the *coming-to-be* of things, at least in certain ancient European regions, Northern and Eastern. It was associated with thunder and lightning in the East, which is an attempt to describe the energetic force of the sky itself as a creative force, which it surely is.

Though the single spiral is more associated with the creative and cyclical-generating nature of the Earth and the Earth's Indweller, the triple "Spinning Spiral" or *triskele* might also be taken to be a symbol of the occurrence, in certain contexts.

"Occurrence" isn't a terribly poetic term. Another term I use for this essential power is "*The Quick*"- which I find more appealing personally. But many names might be poetically created for it, understanding it as I describe it here.

The answer to questions like "where did the basic cosmos-structure itself, with all its natural dynamism, come from?" is both simple, and complex at the same time. The answer is that it didn't come from anywhere; it always was.

And the reason why is because it's not possible for *nothing* to exist. If nothing really had existed (even though "nothing" can't exist precisely because it is nothing) *something* couldn't just one day come from nothing. "Nothing" by its own nature must *lack any capacity*, including the capacity to make something suddenly exist. We know that the world- reality- is real, is there, obviously existing. Thus, it always did exist, in some shape or form.

It's perfectly obvious that the world is dynamic; it is always changing because of the natural dynamism of the cosmos, because of the motion-filled nature of reality. But the great and shocking insight that our investigations of "nothing" reveal is that *reality itself* is uncreated and "unarisen"- this is, in some ways, the greatest wonder of all; things existing and dancing with one another is the eternal baseline of all, *what was always there*.

This perception challenges human minds that insist on believing that "nothing" *had to* proceed "something", or that something or *someone* had to create everything from nothing. But those stories are, simply put, positing a scenario that is impossible. We need not be hindered by them. We must instead take shelter in the wonder of eternal Nature, of things always having been, somehow, at the most fundamental level.

There is a grim amusement that springs forth from any attempt to live this insight in one's life, or embrace it. You will find yourself surrounded by people who sternly reject the idea that nature or the simple reality of all things could have "always been here"- but they will have no issue embracing the idea that a powerful supreme being- himself somehow uncreated- was "always here".

In their minds, a God can exist in some eternal way, a God (conveniently enough) whose name they can invoke for divine sanction upon their aggression, imperialism, and political/social agendas, but *nature itself* in all its wonder and depth cannot have an eternal aspect, cannot have always been here. There mere idea of that is ludicrous to them, somehow.

Needless to say, there is no necessity to create a response to such moronic failures of wit on the parts of such people. Their failures of understanding are part of our modern world brokenness, and any attempt to engage them on such an obviously absurd point as this one will likely fail.

They will not give up on their "eternal God who made nature as an afterthought to his glory at some point later" story because that story (in their minds and the minds of many others) bestows social, political and spiritual authority upon them, and undergirds their empty appeals to their imaginary absolute.

Earth Indweller Mawkin Form

III: The Indweller in the Earth

And from deep spaces and dark, far below, the Earth was full of life.

Here in our world, within the earth and within our sky and our oceans (that world-structure all around us which is "the cosmos" for all effective purposes hereafter as far as I'm concerned) there are certain very powerful *other-than-human persons* whose stories are intimately connected with ours.

The occurrence doesn't, as far as I know, *choose* to do things. It just exists and occurs. As a consequence of its activities, sensing, individually existing persons can come to be. After that, these particulate beings can realize the occurrence or not realize it, or dance along with it, or enjoy it, or whatever they like. They can even ignore it.

Many things that persons do *because* of it are often not recognized as being motivated by it, but wise persons might know. And it's not like we humans *have* to know about the occurrence. It's so close to us, so intrinsically embedded in our very beings (at all levels) that it may simply be a thing that's easy to miss- very much like the field of *Sensation* in this way.

For those aware of Sensation, and wondering how *The Quick* or *The Occurrence* might relate to it, *Sensation* is the very *material* of all reality, and the Occurrence, for me, describes the dynamic nature of all things in reality, composed of that Sensation or the "dark material" that is

Sensation. If Sensation was an ocean of types (and it surely is) then the wave-activity on the ocean and inside it is the Occurrence.

The Occurrence doesn't change somehow just because we know about it or don't know about it, or tell stories about it or make names up for it. It's not necessarily the "most important thing" in the cosmos, but it is very much near the roots of the cosmos, so it's a very fundamental thing. You can't have a cosmos without it.

Now, two very powerful other-than-human Persons in our world came to be. It's fair to say, if rudely pressed for some kind of "explanation", that they came to be through ancient and natural interactions of forces that are obscure to us, but quite obviously involving The Quick somehow, in conjunction with other unguessable powers. These two Indwellers did some things that led to our eventual arising as human beings. They were not the *only* forces that interacted to lead to our arising, but they are two *very* important forces in the chain of interactions that led to humans coming to be as we are now. Along with the simple fact of Sensation and the reality of the Quick, these two Indwellers are the chief authors or sources of our humanity as we experience it now. And they are the sources of the present state of being of many other entities, too.

Our wandering souls- the "free soul" that doesn't die when these bodies do- were in a strange but direct way born from one of these Persons. This may be difficult to talk about, but for the sake of this story, let's just say these souls were born in the same way a human child gestates in a human woman's womb, and finally comes forth when the time is right.

This Motherly Person who is the source of all wandering souls is the Earth Indweller. She Indwells the Earth beneath us. She's the chief powerful person who is at the "center" of the Underworld, if you want to consider it that way; she is the Queen within the interior of all things. But the Underworld isn't really a "thing" with a finite "center" as we ordinarily conceptualize that.

This birth of souls could have happened long before it was possible for anything to live on the surface of the earth- but who knows? Our ordinary conceptions of time aren't central when discussing such things. Either way, the interior dimension of this reality, the Underworld, does has a *chief power*- a Person who has the most influence in that space.

And *She* appears to be a female person; not because She has breasts and a womb, but because She produces things from inside herself, from her own power. From her own power, a natural capacity of her basic being, forces become shaped in certain ways and maintain that shape in some very cohesive way thereafter. In short, She has a power of creation.

She is the source of the "four realms"- the realm of stones, soil, and earth; the realm of plants and growing things like trees; the realm of animals and beasts, and the realm of the human animal, finally. It's not strictly necessary to separate the human animal from the other ones; we share nearly everything with them. All of the entities of the latter three realms (the wandering souls of plants, trees, and animals, and the materials of their bodies) are born directly from the Indweller in the Earth's body.

As I mentioned before, this Great Person exists and has any power She has, ultimately, because of the occurrence. But I don't think She sits around saying "Oh thank you, God-Occurrence for making me; how can I serve you?" That wouldn't make sense, nor be coherent at all.

I can posit that She knows that She arose from a dark chain of interactions and circumstances that I'm guessing human brains cannot fathom, but who can say what She really knows? Or if She even cares? For the sake of simple respect for an Elder, and my own brand of piety, I'm going to just assume that She knows a lot about it, owing to her very powerful and ancient mind.

Now the wandering souls born from Her, they all lived in that space we call the Underworld, and were there for a timelessly long time. Technically, they are still there. They won't ever *not* be there. They have this deep world of their own, a native country or condition closer to the heart of things. All that they need in that world flows from The Indweller-Queen somehow, and that world's natural field of bounty. Their interactions with one another there produce all their own dramas and relationships and their own "history", just like our human interactions here do for us.

And it's a pretty amazing place, at least from the human folkloric and mythological perspective. It has its terrors and its wonders, just like our world does. It is presented as terrible and wonderful by turns, not unlike is ruling Lady. It is presented as possessing a timeless quality and a wholeness that our present experience of our world seems to lack, a thing we shall discuss more shortly. This world is as real as the one we encounter every day with our senses, and at times and in the presence of special conditions, it intersects very strongly with our world.

Around the Earth Indweller are the *Grey Women*- serving-spirits bound to her in deep relationship and intimacy, powerful spirits who mediate both the warm, life-giving powers of the Earth and the blessings of organic life to all persons above, and who perhaps have a role in taking life when the time is proper. They are sometimes the transformed and powerful *Ancestresses* of ancient human lines, but the Ancestresses of non-human beings can be counted among their number, too. The overlap of these Grey Women and the *Fate Women* who are more properly associated with the feminine-associated power of *cosmic necessity* is immense, and they may be a subset of precisely the same powers.

The *Rig Veda* has an interesting verse in it that I will give here, which is relevant to what I just said when I was musing on whether or not the Earth Indweller knew the deepest secrets of her own origin, or the origin of her body the earth, which are completely connected. These verses will also be very relevant to what is said in the coming chapter regarding the Wind or World Indweller. These verses are grappling with the mysterious powers that made the Gods and the world entire:

"There were begetters,

There were mighty forces,
Free action here and energy up yonder;
Who verily knows and who can here declare it,
Whence the world was born,
And whence comes this creation?
The Gods are later than this world's production.
Who knows then whence it first came into being?
He, the first origin of this creation,
Whether he formed it all, or did not form it,
Whose eye controls this world in highest heaven:
He verily knows it, or perhaps he knows not. "

(Hymn CXXIX, verses 5-7)

IV: The Indweller in the Wind of the World

As surely as earth came to be through the natural interplay of cosmic powers at some point, the sky did, too. And there is another Person in this world- The Indweller in the Wind- who did some very important things with regard to the arising of mankind and other forms of life. With this Person, I'm certain we're dealing with a great being who is quite elegantly aware of the power of life-force itself, the great occurrence. Everything he does can be described as a strange and mind-bending *celebration* of the creative force that is natural to this world. He is the Wind Indweller, yes, but also called the "World Indweller" (which is a distinct thing from *Earth Indweller*.)

The Sky, the air enveloping our earth, came to be through its own chain of formational powers, and that phenomenon of air (like the Earth) has its Indwelling Person. This Person decided, at some point long ago, that it was time for *things* to start moving around in different ways, for a quality of *vivification* to take hold on the surface of the land, and as we shall see, even inside it. I don't know *why* He decided this. He might not know why, or maybe He does, but it really doesn't matter.

We never need to know the full story on *how* things came to be to know the things we need to know about what came to be. And the most important question we have to answer for ourselves as human beings is "what's out there with us, and what are the best, wisest, most respectful ways of interacting with them with regard to benefits all

World Indweller Mawkin Form

around?" That's our best question, though I fear we are no longer very good at asking such questions.

The ancient Inuit people have a myth about *Kaila*, also called *Sila*, the Wind Indweller, and His role in motivating the formation of life and new situations on earth. Lines from that myth state "*In the beginning, there was no sun in the sky and the land of those far times was warm and dry... Kaila, He who is Thunder in gray skies, knew it was time to bring life into the land.*" Of course, how He knew "it was time" is not explained, and it need not be.

The Wind Indweller indwells the atmospheric air that surrounds our world. This includes the phenomenon of the winds, and the fiery/electrical discharges that can happen when the air and the earth interact. All of the phenomenon of the air- like storms- fall into His "sphere of presence"; storms are as much a part of His being as a human's emotions are a part of her being, or a song she sings is part of her being.

Like the Earth Indweller and all other powerful spirits or beings, He has a *quality of presence* that can be sensed or experienced by many other beings, in many direct and mysterious ways.

He's a great moving force and very strong- or at least, that's part of the *sensual encounter* with His being, arguably the most primal portion of the encounter. The rage of the wind or the crack of thunder is another tangible example of an encounter with Him. He is of a different nature from the Indweller in the Earth, though they are both offspring of this common nature, this world we all share in common.

In truth, The Wind or World Indweller's being is not limited by anything. It's hard to imagine, but He's like the boundless field of life itself. He's not *the* field, but he Indwells it. And that field appears, again poetically and iconographically as a great light that doesn't have limits. This light, poetically speaking, "pours through" the luminous things we can see, like fire or the sun, but the actual fullness of the light is invisible. It's pretty much everywhere that we can consider, illuminating the great world of life, seen and unseen.

This boundless light and boundless life-field is caused by the occurrence as readily as fire-sparks are caused by sticks rubbing together vigorously; and it *is* the bulk of the most sensual aspect of the occurrence. The Indweller in the Wind or World is very close to the roots of things; He's a very fundamental Person to the world. If there was a single being in our world who *most* manifested the boundless activity of the occurrence through his actions and personality, it would be *Him*.

So He's not the *same* as the occurrence, (even though He couldn't or wouldn't exist without it, just like we wouldn't) but He is as close to the randy, wild, transformative nature of the occurrence as you'll ever come *in the form of a person*.

So he blew things around, vivified things, filled the world with a new kind of motion and life force, and the entities from deep below in the Underworld were very in awe of it, very attracted to it. Some began to "come up" to experience it. They came up, fascinated and attracted by the new light and commotion, and *shifted their shapes* so that they could have a way to be "up here above", and so they could capture the breath of Him.

Shape-shifting is a *cooperative act*; they cooperated with one another and with other powers to share the ability to gain new shapes with each other. To assume a new shape, one needs not just the skill and vitality and motivation- which nearly all spirits and free souls have- but one also (depending on one's destination) needs a *matrix*- a "mother" force to draw the *completion power* of shaping and forming from.

A human mother is only one example of a "matrix" that a free soul might need to complete its full shape-shifting passage into the human world that we know; all free souls gained their earliest shape through the matrix of the Earth Indweller, who is not human and not in possession of a human womb. Something else about her, a thing deeper and stranger, was able to act as a matrix for distinctive living beings. The earth itself (to make another example) along with water and light and air, all together act as matrix to the spirit of a plant seeking to assume a constant green shape.

This brings up interesting questions and speculations about how the Great Powers themselves might shape-shift; could the World Indweller, if he chose, become a bird? Surely he could, by investing part of his power into the egg of a living bird and having that portion of him born in the shape of the bird. To simply *appear* to you or I as a bird at this moment, *without that process*, without tapping into a matrix, would be accomplished differently: He would alter your senses or perceptions, *using your mind as matrix* to give form to him as a vision or a dream that you would encounter and interact with. In the spirit of understanding my own limitations as a mortal with a mortal mind, it's important to admit here that the greatest powers may be able to appear in other ways, too, and perhaps the same can be said of other sufficiently powerful spirits, too. It was long known in human understanding that not every entity we encounter in this world that looks human, is human.

At any rate, the free souls that were coming up and assuming new shapes- those underworldly entities attracted to the display of power here- they wanted to be in this world, in new forms, and to take His wind into themselves, receive His force into themselves, and experience it. They gained *breath souls* for themselves and became living beings as we understand the term in a more ordinary way. Their breath bound them to the surface world, and connected them together.

But a breathing being can't hold on to the breath forever, and can't stay shape-shifted in just one shape forever: the dynamism of the occurrence and the Fateful laws of reality don't allow for the kind of effort it takes to maintain that perpetually. So when they gave up the breath and shifted their shapes at the ends of their lives, they just sank back down to their birth country in the interior of the world, before (sometimes) "flying back up" to do it again.

This whole cycle, I suspect, is *hypnotic* in a way, to them. The breath they come to claim is intoxicating to them. The breath itself is *exhilarating* somehow. It changes how they experience themselves and their world. It gives them the power to have new kinds of perceptions- to reason things as you and I reason, and to measure things as you and I measure. But with it comes what you might call a list of "pros and cons."

You and I, as we are now, can stand by a swimming pool, take a deep breath and dive down. Under that water it's surreal-looking and everything is weird and distorted. Then, we start to hurt for air after a time and finally, we come back up, leaving that weird world below behind and getting more air from up here in the clear, sharp, straight world.

That's exactly what's happening to our wandering souls, except *reversed*. The wandering soul's natural home is a surreal, weird world deep below, and souls that feel compelled to come and live in this "world above" are "diving up" to get air. They breathe it as long as they can before having to give up, breathe it out, and go back down- either through the passage of enough time, or through an interaction that forces them to give the breath up at some other point before that.

This world that seems so rational and ordinary to you and me, so clear, so full of lines and defined spaces- it's the weird one to *Them*. It might be fair to say that this breathy world, and the breath that connects them to it and to each other (and all other living things) is like their "trip".

So the Wind Indweller delights in his activities here, and he is the source of breath souls- and an Earth Indweller dwells below who is the source of free or wandering souls. It is a meeting of the potencies of the *earth/underworld and sky* that makes us "what we are" in our present experience. We are partly of the waters below, of the abyss, and partly of the winds above.

Some people, in the distant past and in the present, have often depicted these two Indwelling entities as a *God* and a *Goddess*, though that's just a particular cultural language. She has been often called an *Earth Mother* (rightly, for the she really fits that description quite well) and He has been called (among other things) a *Sky Father*- but the situation isn't that simple. This *religious urge* to depict them in such a way is again, part of various historical cultural impulses. It's just as fair to call them "very powerful spirits" or Persons of an extraordinary or ancient variety. It's just as fair to call them "Grandmother" and "Grandfather", or even "Great Grandmother" and "Great Grandfather."

It should be obvious by now that souls didn't "come here" alone; they didn't emerge from the depths and take shape here alone. They weren't born alone; no soul has ever really been alone, and no soul can every *truly* be alone. They related to one another in the deep or in the Unseen before this world became full of life and full of new pathways for them. And they- *we*- relate here still.

There is a natural and intrinsically-resident instinct within us *to help one another to thrive and survive*. It extends from a world or a condition of being older than this one. It extends from the deepest reality of kinship, which finds its provenance in the womb of the common Grandmother of all life.

Social fictions, social delusions and social confusions *can* and *will* obscure our grasp of that instinct, and our power to act on it as we should, but it remains nonetheless. The insane deeds and mistreatments that we heap upon one another, all born in the disconnected field of aggression, alienation and confusion that is characteristic of our civilized modern day will obscure that instinct too.

This instinct doesn't only manifest an urge to help the beings most like us (other humans) to thrive and survive; we are kin to other-than-human beings too, of many varieties, and that sense of kin-feeling naturally extends to them as well, at least in the hearts and minds of all sane and wise people. Non-human creatures overwhelmingly came to inhabit this world in many shapes long before we humans did. They are natural elders to us.

V. He Went Into the Earth

The Wind or World Indweller has a plenitude of power in this world. For all practical purposes, it wouldn't be unfair to consider him something like "all powerful" with regards to the physical, measurable universe. The Earth Indweller, on the other hand, appears to have the lion's share of power in the dark spaces "outside" of this world: The Netherworld, or the Unseen. What kinship He has with our breath souls, She has with our wandering souls.

While we live in this world, His movements and motions (and the ways He may become dangerous or wrathful at times) should concern us quite a bit: nature's storms and violent, energetic motions can topple cities and even civilizations. We are, in a sense, "under his power" while living in this world. But in death, when the breath soul is released and dissolves back into the wind and sky it came from and only the wandering soul remains, we come "into Her power", she being the source-mother of the wandering soul's origin. In death, we come under the powers that are *deeper*, in the Underworld, the powers that are Ancestral. While we live and breathe, the deeper forces do still influence us, but chiefly through visions, dreams, intuitions, and the like. They *can* go further than that, of course, but it's rare these days.

Reality being what it is, there are no neat divisions. What I've described here thus far is as truthful as I can manage, but if you thought it sounded a bit too neat and well-divided, you might have good instincts. At some point (it is said) He, the Wind Indweller, also went into the earth, into

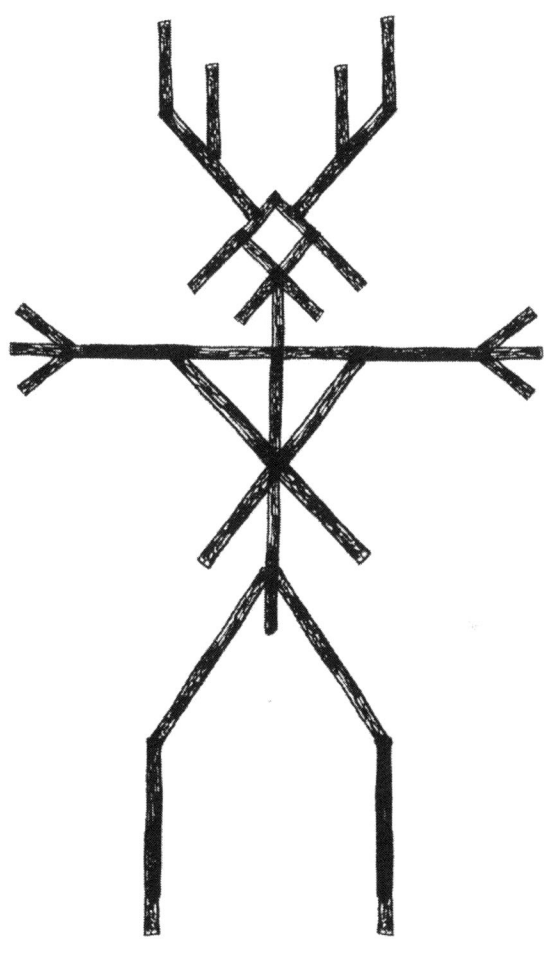

Chthonic World Indweller Mawkin Form

the Below, and wandered into or filled the ground and the caves below, and even penetrated into the further Depths. This is a parallel to how he (in the breath) fills the earthy bodies of living creatures and dwells in the "caves" and hollows of our bodies. He thus remains merged with the greater Land itself, *Her* body. He is not merely an atmospheric person, but an earthy or *chthonic* one as well.

This is why he appears in so much folklore and in so many of the myths of earlier religions as a mysterious chthonic and land-based figure, not just a sky or air-based presence. So great is the aesthetic distinction between the realm of sky and the realm of earth, that we see in the evolution of myth (in nearly all places) *two distinct Gods often forming from this*: a fatherly, usually more severe and distant "Sky" God, and a more sensual, wild, tricky, or dangerous "Earth" God or spirit, who might be his son and sometimes his adversary.

The division between the Wampanoag Native American supernatural figure *Hobbomock* (the strange, sensual, earth-based, stormy sorcerer/tutelary Devil-Spirit, who manifests primarily in the ghostly form of dead people, snakes, and antlered creatures) and his "counterpart", the far more distant creator God *Cautantowwit*, who was "seen by humans not at all" in visions or dreams, is an example of this same thing.

It is worth noting that the Narragansett and Wampanoag (probably in common with all New England tribes, and other tribes besides) held a distinction between the wandering soul/free soul- which they called *cowwewonck*, or the "dream soul", which was derived from their word *cowwene*, meaning "to sleep", and which became active when a person was in a trance or asleep- and a second soul, the *michachunk*, the "soul of a higher notion", which was associated with "clear sight" or "discerning." It bestowed upon a person the capacity of discernment or of measuring, and of ordinary sight; it was the breath soul.

It was known among the natives that these two souls did not follow the same course at death. The dream soul of a person or a sorcerer/shaman could remain on earth after death to act as a helper to other sorcerers. Hobbomock was associated, in this strange capacity, with the dream-soul, and those in alliance with him in life could "appear   and disappear in many forms "like images in a dream" after death.

Hobbomock's other name *Cheepi*, refers to the dream-soul of departed dead humans. As William S. Simmons writes in his seminal work *Spirit of the New England Tribes*, "The dream soul, *cowwewonck*, would seem to be the entity known after death as *Cheepi*, the Shaman's helper, and also to have shown (itself) at times as a light in the evening sky."

Because of the metaphysical penetration of the Wind Indweller into the ground and into the realm of chthonic and tellurian matters, and because of the universal perception on the parts of humans that "earth is fertilized by its mating with the sky", many depict the Wind Indweller and the Earth Indweller as a married couple or as mates. In most ways, that's very fair. This is the source of the mythical icon/motif of the *marriage of heaven and earth*, but this motif is not crucially important to gaining a deeper understanding of these entities, in my view. Cultures will present marriages and mates in various culturally-conditioned ways, and those ways don't always take well to two such immense and strange beings as the Earth and Wind Indwellers. Cultural language can be quite limited. I view these Indwellers as distinct-but-relating persons and powers, each of whom acted in certain ways, expressed powerful capacities, and otherwise did things that made our human lives (and countless other lives) possible. They are the *Foreparents*, and remain so.

It was His great light, and His great power, His breath, that attracted strange entities "up here"- to manifestation- from the deep. I don't know if He meant for that to come to pass, or if He knew that it would. Again, maybe He did, maybe He didn't. In the wise spirit of respect, I will assume that he did. I don't really believe that this particular event was the entire "point" of our existence, however, a thing planned out in the long-term by other powers: for souls to wander up here and get breath and live as humans or deer or cats. It may have just been a thing that happened, a strange serendipity, or a thing that happens from time to time in some larger cycle that we know nothing about.

The more I think on it, the more I believe that the "point" of the existence of the wandering souls was simply that a motherly force (and other forces, too) brought about the conditions that allowed them to exist as they did. They had (and presently have) this infinite, dark and surreal space to dwell in, which is their natural space. That space appears, to us humans, to be "deep down" inside of things, including ourselves. And it's not time-limited, at least, not in any ordinary sense. *Organically coming to be and interacting* is a sufficient description of the reality of any life.

That some of the entities in the deep were attracted to the great commotion up above, and the new wild wind-ride, might have nothing at all to do with the earlier "generation" of wandering souls that came about in the boundless deep. Again, breathing life as we ordinarily know it may be a pure serendipity of interacting powers, and not part of a great plan with regards to these lives.

Now, if you believe in Fate, (and I do) Fateful forces operating deep in the background might have seen to it that certain powers got near one another at just the right time to bring about certain conditions that they desired for some reason- who can say?

I do think that these sorts of ponderings are really outside of the scope of this present work, but important ponderings nonetheless. I have no issue believing the obvious truth that, once certain forces come together, fateful consequences must follow: if you take the breath of life, you must give it up, eventually. Death is part of the Fate of the living. Beyond that, I can't say with certainty how involved other, deeper powers are in why the daily particularities of things come about. I suspect the answer to such a question would bend our minds into oblivion if we really obtained it.

VI: The Ancient Serpent with a Million Eyes

The Wind Indweller- the Master Spirit of this World- ("spirit" here is meant in the basic sense of "*spiritus*", which means "wind") moves about all the time, driven by the Quick. He does this or He does that, and He wanders around everywhere. Through His breath and life-force that is within all living things, He fills all with fecundity, desires, motivations, animation and urges.

The real and ultimate source of those urges is naturally the Quick. What motivates the greatest powers motivates us all; but we gain our access to these forms of life and our power to sensually enjoy those urges in this world (and our occasions to suffer them) through the activities and the previous/ongoing deeds of the Indwellers, and other powers besides them. We never live, walk, or experience alone by our own power, and we certainly never die alone.

The World Indweller was depicted as a *Great Serpent* by many of the ancients. This is a very important symbol because the serpent is the basic symbol or form of life-force itself. In the minds of the ancients, the serpent was the simplest form of life: just a long, simple body and a head, without limbs. Serpents have a phallic shape, a shape associated with fecundity, sex, and desire. And serpents shed their skin, renewing themselves, as the seasons get renewed or as birth renews humans and other creatures. The serpent as a basic symbol for life force is met by the egg as a symbol for the Earth Indweller's power of creation.

As a symbol of basic life-force, the serpent "coils" like the DNA strands in us coil around. All of these things overlap in an ancient, symbolic language. Life, and the chain of life, is like a serpent, a great serpentine power.

The re-emergence of this "Serpent Power" in the land was viewed as responsible for the seasonal re-greening of the earth in many traditional cultures in the past; the legendary *Green Man* figure is rooted in nothing other than the Master Spirit of this world in an anthropomorphic form, representing that power coming forth again- "The God Who Comes."

By being in the Land and in all breathing things, the Master Spirit has "A Million Eyes" because he's able to see, in a way, through your eyes and mine. *He Indwells our breath souls*, and as a consequence, human wandering souls come under his power or influence, too, for a time. This is the paradox: such a powerful, "huge" cosmological being is still *somehow individual* and local, too- he is "localized" through the distinct phenomenon of the breath of even the smallest of creatures. He is able to be related to, in ways, by individuals.

But because He is in the ground and in the land, He "sees" in hills, or trees, too. Or in a fox, or a squirrel, or in other entities that we can't see, but who are there. The sun long ago became associated with one of His eyes, and the moon (in some places) His other eye- one eye (the sun) to see in this world, and the other (the moon) to "see in the unseen", which the world of night represents. But the sun has a longer history of being associated with the World or Wind Indweller than most other heavenly phenomenon.

Because of His presence in the ground and in all creatures, the animals of the world- the beings of the forest, the wild beasts- mythically (and actually) "obey" him, or He has some influence over how they may act. Thus it is that his "chthonic" and earthy form- often in which he appears as a part-animal/part-human hybrid, and particularly as a horned man- is associated with forests and animals. This is the image of the God or Master of sylvan places and beasts, the Hunter, the Woodman or Wood-Ward, the Master of Animals.

This ancient "horned god" icon, and the way it came to inform the Christian belief in the Devil having an animalistic and horned shape, should concern us here. The Witchfather creates the capacity for witchcraft in people *through gifting them with familiar spirits that appear in animal shape*. I believe those spirits are not randomly assigned, but reflect a pre-existing relationship the awakening sorcerer or witch has with their ancestral fetch-follower, though other familiar spirits later obtained might not exist in previous relationship to the witch. The Master in this capacity is the "*Granter of the Boon of the Familiar*", the Witch-Initiator *par excellence*.

I am always saying "The World is Full of Eyes." The great eye, or the Horned Eye, is the World Indweller's symbol. The sun is like His great eye, but the *eye itself* is a sign of the Indwelling Intelligence of Nature, which is Him. So the "Ancient Serpent with a Million Eyes" is a circumlocution for the Master Spirit of this world, the Witchfather, the Sorcerer and Sorceress-teacher considered in his closer, more intimate "chthonic" and terrestrial hypostasis.

He has as many names as he has eyes. And I believe that His

level of nigh-omniscient awareness, a consequence of His merging with the ground and living beings and so forth, means that His attentions are *very easy* to gain, all things considered. I think He can hear and see nearly everything. He is the entity that John Grigsby refers to as The *Universal Daimon*.

I think that at this point, the further layers of meaning in the verse I gave earlier from the *Rig Veda* is much clearer now:

"He, the first origin of this creation,
Whether he formed it all, or did not form it,
Whose eye controls this world in highest heaven:
He verily knows it, or perhaps he knows not."

It can come as no surprise that the source of breath souls Himself, and the many powers connected to him, are responsible not only for the process of granting breath and of motivating the course of life through lust and vital exuberance, but also responsible in some ways for the process of the *separation and reclaiming* of breath. Thus, they are involved in the Fateful events relating to death.

The Master as Hunter of Souls- the leader of the fearful "Wild Hunt" that appears universally across Eurasia and in many other places, is a reference to the World Indweller's presence in destructive or terrifying storms connected to his habits as hunter- and not just hunter of beasts, but hunter of *all who must die*, including humans. Nature's predatory, threatening side is brought forward in the icon of the Wild Hunter, and historically, even certain human beings have been chosen through a special spiritual vocation to become

Involved in the Wild Hunt, even before their own deaths. Freed from their bodies temporarily, their free souls joined the Hunter's "Wild Rout" through the sky and through the Unseen. During these times, they were compelled by Fate- while being led by Him- to participate in the chain of fateful consequences that led to the deaths of man and beast.

These *choosers of the slain*, the arrow-hurling women and men who were sometimes forcibly joined to the Wild Hunt, were often accused by authorities of using witchcraft to murder people. In reality they were simply joining with the fateful cavalcade of invisible powers that were *already coming to take the people they saw killed*, even if they perceived their own hands doing the killing in their visionary state. It was a *death-divination vision*, given from other, deeper powers- from the Master of the Hunt and the aerial Fate-Women, the Deathly Women who manifest lethal doom from the Unseen, and other lethal powers besides.

The powerful Isobel Gowdie and her death-divination Covenant were drawn in this way into the Master's company, the *Company of the Storm*, the fateful death-dealing Wild Hunt, to take part in this ancient phenomenon. She was likely murdered by her society for this participation, and for the witchcraft she practiced otherwise, in alliance with other spirits.

The Unseen, and all entities within it, can take on a predatory aspect. Predation is natural, sacred, and normal. It is how power is *freed, changed, and transferred* between the human and beast-world/foliate world, and between the human and beast worlds, and the world of spirits.

VII: The Ravenous Tide and the Motif of "Otherworldly Rescue."

At this point, I must make a shift away from pure explorations of cosmology and mingle cosmology with some thoughts on eschatology that I hope won't be too burdensome or overdone, as so much eschatological thinking in the past has been in my view.

For the longest time, life in this world went on just as you'd expect, with these great powers we've talked about interacting, with humans interacting with them and with other spirits and beasts and one another, and the world-urge driving things along. Living beings *rose up* and went *back down* in great numbers; the seasons came and went. But then, at a certain point, it's safe to say that our human wandering souls ran into some very dark problems.

At first- and for countless ages of time- these souls assumed their earthly forms, took breath into themselves, lived, died, sank back down, and were at peace with the coming and the going. Some souls or beings lived and became n*ew kinds of spirits* after that life or perhaps after many "lives"- a new category of immortal spirit-entities that *still exist*, wise beings who no longer mindlessly fly back and forth between Underworld and Aboveworld, and who cannot be compelled to seek new shapes and experiences in any intoxicated or mindless way.

I think that these spirits, these entities, can teach us much if we find them and relate to them. I know that they bestowed help on humans in long ages past. They haunt our legends from all over the world: the wild men and women in the forest, part animal, part human, sometimes terrifying and sometimes beautiful or wondrous in their appearances.

I believe that they became that way through making relationships with the Master Spirit, as their horned, bestial, wild shapes would indicate. These would be the entities I call (and folklore calls) the Hobbs. They still exist now, though they are considered demons by many. As helping and tutelary spirits to humans in many capacities and for many ages, they took (in later times) the roles of tutelary spirits to secret covenants and groups of sorcerers and witches who were devoted to the Master. As the Master's true "ministers", there is nothing in their appearance, personalities, or level of wisdom that does not reflect the Master's "magistry" perfectly.

With the new possibilities of mind and experience made possible through the vicissitudes of life and breath, I think that other beings became other kinds of entities. When I call them immortal, I don't mean to insinuate that the free soul isn't already immortal; I just mean Immortal in a *new way*. The wandering soul may already be immortal, but it *can* be afflicted by a kind of intoxication or confusion. These new immortals simply developed the needed wisdom and shape-shifting ability to avoid excess amounts of the mental confusion and limitations that might mark other beings, and which cyclically disrupts the minds, memories, and personalities of those beings.

The Master's wild, potent, bright and alluring presence- and the attraction of beings to it- it made new things possible:

new events, new vistas, and new experiences. These serendipitous or incredible "surprise combinations" of power and force in the kaleidoscope of the cosmos may be one of the most understated but important qualities of the world of life. If you get new mixtures of forces and circumstances, there's always a possibility for the arising of even new classes of beings.

For countless ages, life went on just this way. But then, a very strange (and for us, and many other creatures, a not-so-great thing) happened. In the vast body of Fate, the darker, deeper texture of reality, you might say there are *ripples*- Like waves on the ocean's surface. These "ripples" or tides, they extend from an infinitely deeper level of the cosmos-structure than I have been talking about in this work before now. It's fair to say that the Indwellers themselves might seem "small" compared to these great waves or ripples or tides.

As these waves come and go, the world and all things otherwise become impacted and affected. Metaphysical realities that might not have had such an influence on our world or on living beings before might begin to have an impact on them. If I had to categorize these tides in terms of cosmos-structure, they are nearly at the same fundamental level as the *occurrence* is. If we consider our earth as having seasons, these "tides" from deeper levels might represent huge seasons for the greater cosmos which is beyond our conception.

So, every now and again, a ripple or a tide comes through, and they can bring about dark, weird things. Perhaps some can destroy entire worlds. No matter what they bring, no matter what strange or subtle atmosphere they might eventually bring to bear on our earth or the world of our experience, the Master Spirit is wise enough and powerful enough *to ride any wave*. He can shift his shape, like the master Shape Shifter/Turnskin He is, and adapt to any change, no matter where it is from. And He can do it whether He "likes" what the wave or tide is requiring Him to do, though I'd guess he probably doesn't look at things that way. He is the Master of adaptations, and so are his Hobbs, and other similarly wise and powerful spirits.

Humans, however, are not nearly so good at this feat of shape-shifting at the mental level, or the physical one. A dark "tide" that made this world rapidly uninhabitable wouldn't trouble the Master or His Hobbs, nor would it threaten quite a few other spirits, but I think the rest of us humans and animals (and many other beings) would end up like a school of a million fish that drown off the shore of Peru when some toxic algae gets washed into a particular bay by a larger current of the ocean.

A *deeper Fateful tide* moved in and brought its presence to bear on our world. How localized this tide was, or if it was something greater, I have no way of knowing nor do I need to know. I'd consider its power to be pretty terrible, speaking as a human being at my present level of wisdom and awareness. I call it the Red *Tide or* the Ravenous *Tide* because it seems to have infected mankind with a sort of terrible hunger, a subtle mix of anxiety and ravenous hunger for things they had never before focused upon with the same ardor or intensity.

Chthonic World Indweller: The Hunter
Predation Binds Man, Beast, and Spirit

You might say that what emerged through them was a kind of selfishness or greed gone mad, but it came down to humans *creating a new way of living in this world* which culminated into a full blown worldwide phenomenon at one point in history. It was (and is) a way of living that was more of a *trap* than any sort of sane or agreeable way of life.

At this point, I'd like to make it clear that I am talking about the *true* "Fall of the Human World" event- not the many popular "fall of man" versions of this idea that are so prominent, and which get so moralistically convoluted or used to justify the creation of institutionalized religions. I'm talking about a *historically-backed perception and fact* that at one point, technological changes and other changes brought about worldwide institutions of *civilization*, which represented radical departures from how humans had lived before for countless hundreds of thousands of years.

With civilization came a *departure* from the primordial life-way of the original forager peoples, from their spontaneous acceptance of the spirit-saturated and spirit-haunted worlds, and their near-zero environmental impact on the world, and *an entry into more organized, controlled, and institutionalized existence.* This came with the presence (for the first time) of highly organized violence in the service of states, and massive wealth disparity and wealth stratification which rapidly caused the formation of social classes.

People have wondered for a long time what could have caused this shift. We know that the discovery of agriculture and the domestication of plants was the main technological (and obvious) reason for civilization's establishment and perpetuation. But in suggesting that a deeper Fateful shift occurred, not planned by any known or knowable entities, I am attempting to answer the question in a deeper way.

I am attempting to avoid the "flaw" arguments that point to a defect or blame in man or a menace of any conceivable spiritual proportions. I say that humans in one or two places simply experienced a fateful shift in how they considered the realities of their survival and prosperity and began attempting strategies of food production and storage that ended up being, in the long-run, a very dangerous and bad idea, and one that eventually spilled incredible amounts of blood.

They didn't *choose* to fall into greedy habits of systematically controlling land and domesticating plants and animals; they simply got some initial benefits from so doing, and couldn't return to a more free (and to their eyes, more risky) way of being. They became afraid of risk and wanted more predictability. They loved the power that excess and surplus brought. They loved the feeling of security and eventually of prestige that came from having so much.

And they began to destroy the forests for cropland and pastureland. They began to kill *en masse*- they caused the deaths of many other beings and many other humans. They killed for the control of plants and animals, and they killed to domesticate plants and animals. They killed for minerals. They invented castes, slavery, worker classes, and through their efforts, poverty and injustice for most beings alive was inevitable. The massive population surge born of agricultural surplus was also inevitable, and that leads us directly into the modern (and quite hard to sustain) modern industrial world.

I must mention at this point that in the vocabulary of most people alive today, the word civilization has a very positive connotation. This is not an accident. We view "civilized" as the *obvious, normal, and unquestionably positive way of being* in this world. Contrasted to *uncivilized*, the distinction couldn't be more massive: the "uncivilized" are thought brutal, vicious, unclean, dirty, and unsophisticated. Ironically, however, the most brutal efforts ever taken to kill or subjugate human beings and other living creatures, and the most devastating, disruptive cultural activities ever pressed against the soul of this world, have all been the works and deeds of civilizations and civilized people.

It is very important to understand that human beings existed for most of their history in a pre-civilized state. Civilization is not the only way that we can exist on Earth, and it is not, historically speaking, the most common way we have existed before now.

Before civilization, humans had art, kinship groups, language, songs, music, clothing, crafts, sacred stories, religions, sports, and high degrees of cultural sophistication. Civilization is not required for humans to satisfyingly manifest all of the natural powers and urges of their souls. But civilization does bring about new possibilities and new desires which nothing but civilization can satisfy. What the cost to the world might be for all this, however, is another question that we never ask enough.

Civilization requires just one thing: large enough populations, gained through the surplus food produced by agriculture, to create *cities*, which are the hallmark and chief sign-post of the presence of a civilization. And with cities come all of the new wonders- and new terrors- of civilization.

We know that the Master's very presence in us, the power that the wind or air has to bestow these reasoning and measuring (and cunning) minds upon us, has its dangers. In the PGM literature, the Master is described as the "*clandestine one that inhabits every soul in secret*"- because He indwells all breath souls- but it is also said of Him that:

"You (Master) also come and bring delights and pains
Sometimes with reason, sometimes with madness;
Because of you men dare beyond what is fitting for their souls
And they take refuge in your light, which is darkness."

From this, I understand that the basic human mind we are possessed of, under the force of the breath, is itself *wily*- it has an element of rascality, its own little devilish way of wanting to take risks and exceed boundaries that perhaps it shouldn't. This is a reflection of a part of the Master's own character, He who is known for His own antics and strange, sometimes chaotic or frightening behaviors.

But very powerful and very free beings *always* have a way of shocking our notions of how "things" should be. It wasn't the cunning, devious qualities of mind given us by the Master through breath that led to the downfall of the human world; they may have played a small role; we can never rule that out (and when it comes to exceeding boundaries, you can be sure they did) but ultimately, It was a matter of a larger, deeper Fateful season of dark power coming to bear upon the situation of man.

So, the world changed. Souls coming from below to gain breath from here and take shape here found themselves in strange new situations of deep pain, being trapped by the human insanity that was proliferating here above. The pain of this new human world was soul-deep. Life- human life and otherwise- had become reduced to the status of a mere resource to be blithely sliced down like grain for the greedy gain or benefit of others. This shock cut into souls; it pressed deeply into them.

Many souls became (and remain) confused; they became lost and began wandering aimlessly in pain or shock or bewilderment. In short, the red cost of the new age of civilization echoed not just through the well-hacked up and divided-up landscape, but into the Spirit world, as well.

Many humans did great evils and became estranged from other powers. Many humans, because of their insane deeds, became lost in death, unable to effortlessly return to the Ancestral powers below, when they had harmed so many of them here up above. They changed into dangerous entities, desperate and spiteful in their lostness, in this world, and beyond it.

Civilization's basic and fundamental roots, its basic assumptions, must be considered in terms of their benefits, but also in terms of the spiritual and tangible menace that they present to the world, and to humans who fall under the deep conditioning of civilized assumptions.

The human social world up here above became- and remains- terribly unjust, with a pernicious, nigh-omnipresent lack of meaningful connections between humans, a surfeit of greed and violence, and almost no meaningful connection between humans and the Unseen. As ugly as it may be to see it all laid out in this way, we must see; we must comprehend it and accept the problem for what it is.

The "new order of the ages" effectively interrupted the ability of humans to relate to the Unseen or to keep ongoing, intimate contact with other non-human persons. More and more malnourished attempts at the civilized versions of "religion"- attempts to *formalize and control* what was an organic and spontaneous reality for humans in ages before- started to proliferate worldwide. What was once living and fresh became rote and calcified. What once celebrated the open freedom and strangeness of life now celebrated civilization and gave divine justification to its excesses.

The vast majority of human beings born into civilization today don't know anything about what I'm describing here, because the humans inside of civilization created very predictable and underhanded justification stories about themselves and where their civilizations came from. They used the vehicle of the *new kinds of myths* they created and the new structures of religion to erect cognitive traps, or perhaps "understanding snares", that maintain the illusion of the absolutely unquestionable and providential goodness and rightness of civilization. Civilization can never get over its own greatness;

it knows, and it makes certain that its people (and victims) know, that it is the greatest thing that ever happened in the history of human events. No one has ever had it "better." That's the story.

This story and its concomitant illusions are naturally both to the benefit of the true (and very wealthy) human lords of civilization, who benefit greatly from all this, while the vast majority of people remain in the very small places duly assigned to them by cultural choreography and civilized programming.

But the Master, and other spirits (like His Hobbs), and the Earth Indweller, and other powers- they come from a time *unimaginably long* before this tragic and recent turn of events, which we can conclusively state, historically and archaeologically, saw its beginning only 10-12,000 years ago. Though recent civilizations fight to establish themselves as the cornerstones of all history, it is the secret history of *ages upon countless ages* before them which is the true story of breathing men and women and the strange spirits they are, born from the company of other and mightier spirits, ancestral to them and otherwise.

It is my firm belief that the Great Powers took pity on the lost wandering souls that were having to weather this age of the Ravenous Tide. And it is my belief that they attempted various means and modes of "rescue" for those souls.

But have a care in understanding what I mean: this is no attempt to create another version of a story about a "fallen world of sin" that heavenly beings need to come and rescue suffering souls from. If anything, this story is the real and true story- the lost original story- that underpins the various human mythical expressions of a *fallen world*.

This is a world in the grip of a dark season which has proliferated confused souls, and the rescue of the Unseen comes not in simply "carrying human souls away to a better world", or (Powers forbid) a "more true" world, but in awakening a memory and clarity in souls that allows them to rediscover comfort with themselves and this world, and then to find their way with ease into its deeper regions. This rescue involves a revitalized spirit of kinship with the forgotten powers of our origins, wherein natural wholeness and wisdom blossom naturally and easily.

In short, this rescue is a restoration of ease with living and dying, alongside the natural biological and relational wisdom that humans may have had before the hedges of super-division were planted by warlike, controlling, and conquest-minded civilizations.

But it is still a form of rescue, of extraordinary aid, so that's what I call it. I am talking about very cunning and compassionate acts on the parts of spiritual beings, intended to reach out to suffering, lost humans. These would be the very acts of spontaneous and understandable compassion that powerful beings who are directly kin to us- and easily wise enough to understand the importance of freedom- *would be expected to attempt.* It's no strange notion that kinship-bonds and organic connections between beings should inspire such aid from the deep, in many shapes.

"Them in the Unseen" established, through mystical forms of reaching out to living people, things that ancient societies called *mysteries* to help bring people inside of civilization back to an awareness of the spiritual truths that were present and easy to access before civilization. There is a very real and obvious reason why mystery cults of the kind I'm describing here *only appear inside of civilized societies*, but never in pre-civilized primal societies, some of which still exist in various dogged forms even now.

All mysteries, when studied (based on what we can know of them) reveal similar conclusions and similar hoped-for transformations. They all seem to speak of a genuine sideways step, a transformation from one kind of living and being to another- a doorway into another world, into another state, into another metaphysical status, which, in the world of Classical civilizations, was often conceptualized as *and* experienced as a new kind of intimate friendship with the Gods and with the Dead. The culmination of the mysteries represented a *restoration of older, deeper relationship-systems* that the coming of civilization intervened upon.

Other sorts of rescue motifs involve wise teachers or prophets believed to come from beyond, revealing ways of attaining a lost righteousness, of attaining *mokshas* or Nirvana; ways of obtaining transcendent mind states of some sort or wise mind-states that free people from suffering, or even perhaps union with a transcendent absolute.

Many of these sorts of rescue conceptualizations aren't born in the machinations of the Unseen world (though their adherents might beg to differ on that) but are *outgrowths themselves of civilization and civilized philosophies and abstractions*, born in civilized assumptions about the world. But at their core, some of them do seem to stem from a genuine primordial memory-point in which a genuine "rescue attempt" may have been present.

We can easily see in some modern and prominent religions traces of what might be described as very obscure metaphysical and archaeo-psychological remains- and often very misunderstood remains- of true primordial "rescue efforts" which we know do not function at present to bring about authentic metaphysical or spiritual reparation or relief to anyone (assuming they ever did.) Whatever distant grace they intended, or whatever long-faded arcane symbolic systems they might still contain, are not things understood to any depth by the people involved in these religions.

Nevertheless, the traces of these old symbolic languages that no one comprehends at present and of spiritual icons that can't speak their real language to modern people, still reveals the "tracks" of the Spirits that might have reached out once. Some may wonder- and I consider it completely fair to ask- why the compassion or power of the Unseen cannot effectively reach many of those who belong to modern religions like Christianity or Islam.

The answer lies in how both Christianity and Islam are completely undergirded and enslaved by unquestioned civilized tenets. Their religions are outgrowths- perhaps the *chief* outgrowths- of civilization's "political and social centralization urge", writ spiritual. No institutions on earth beyond global capitalism have as much investment in supporting the civilized paradigm for all people as these two religions. Being central outgrowths of the same civilizations that enslave souls would be enough by itself, but these powerful revealed religions went several pernicious steps further. They have intentionally shaped civilizations to fear and hate diversity; they support anti-social and anti-diversity agendas on every front. The Master Spirit of this world is styled a "devil" by both Christianity and Islam on account of his wild and free nature and his refusal to fit into neat and non-threatening conceptions, and the free spirits of the wild and the Unseen are all styled as demons.

The very concept of "wild" underlies a grim metaphysic of evil in these religions, associated as it is with willfulness, selfishness, and disobedience. Even the *truly free depths* at the core of each human being, each human instinct and each human heart are styled as flawed, dangerous places: possible dens for devils and temptations that humans must never pay attention to.

Nature itself, associated with the divine feminine, is subjected to ownership, oppression, violent control, and rape at the hands of human societies with the full sanction of the God of both Bible and Koran. And human women (not surprisingly) universally fall into similar dark Fates at the hands of all societies that Christianity or Islam have historically maintained any controlling or ruling authority within.

Within this condition of rock-hard adherence to pro-civilization conformity, sanctioned by false spiritual glamour, gained through violence and spiritual imperialism and upheld by complex systems of social brainwashing and control, the chances of any compassionate spirit being able to break through on any level to the majority of Christians or Muslims is very slender. The atheists they leave behind them, those ruined souls of people turned off (wisely) by the madness these revealed religions have subjected the world to, are likewise broken to an extent that makes communion on their part with the Unseen world very unlikely. Atheists are the living corpses left behind by the murdering machines of revealed religions, which mutilate and murder souls as readily and regularly as they murder physical bodies in some places.

Christianity and Islam almost completely destroyed the Mystery cults and religions, though it is safe to say that even many of the hallowed mysteries of antiquity had gone into various stages of decay in the final eras of most Pagan civilizations. Most of the ancient doors leading back into the Forests and Meadows of the Unseen were closed by then, and are closed now for good... or at least closed until something else unexpected occurs that might induce a few of the old doors to be opened, or create new doors that might open. Such occasions will be rare.

I am overjoyed to be able to report (in the midst of all this somewhat grim talk) that thanks to the *encoding of important symbols and their related patterns of action* in certain ancient folktales and stories that we are fortunate to be in possession of, a few potent keys to certain old doors *were* preserved. These patterns of action have been given forms of outward actualization/expression by certain esoterically insightful people who have lived before. The sacred activity of searching for and revitalizing these *precious keys* continues in the activities of certain people alive today, including myself, and many of the greatest students of sorcery and the mysteries that I know, and upon whom I rely steadily.

Certain people before us- the giants upon whose shoulders we surely all stand- found ways of regenerating these potent but hidden things. Some mystery-portals are still open. Beyond them lie the rarely-trod green fields of another world (that world which is the very soul of this one) and the dark spaces and endless forests of that same eldritch home of ours, teeming with opportunities for wisdom, power-acquisition, and renewal for our souls.

And we need it; more than ever, we need it. The contents of the rediscovered and regenerated mysteries which I will discuss here soon as well as I may are divided by me into two "branches", essentially divided between those mysteries relating to the Master Spirit himself, and those more properly falling into greater sympathy with the Earth Indweller's being. I believe that both of these Mighty Ones interacted either directly or through their bound agents and serving-daimons with earlier human beings to lay the foundations of many mysteries. Their signatures are clearly stamped upon the two specific soul-and-destiny transformation mysteries that I shall discuss herein.

But before we can begin those explorations (or at least glance at my notes on the first of the two) we have to come to grips with an issue that is admittedly hard for us to accept and process in our own minds here in our modern day. That issue is the idea of the *radical insufficiency* of our ordinary modern-day human lifestyles with regard to creating beneath us *any form of grounding* that might make us able to really comprehend the full essence of the mysteries. We must comprehend how impoverished our ordinary lives in this world have made our basic grasp of *what genuine wisdom really is*, or what it might mean in a larger, more expansive or deeper sense. Admitting that we may have major handicaps or deficits in these matters is hard for most people to do. However, I think few things can be more important if we are serious about attaining to the sorts of transformations we really might need.

No matter who we are, because of how we live and because of the horror show that has our minds and brains and souls in its steel grip, it is not unfair to say that we are nearly hopelessly lost in the face of comprehending the subtle depths that describe the true nature of ourselves and our reality. Real wisdom and insight is as rare for you and me as finding a particular grain of sand on a beach somewhere.

No matter how well that grain of sand might be described, and even if we were allowed to look at a very detailed picture of it, our chances of finding it on even a small beach wouldn't be that great. To imagine that any wisdom we can produce of our own lonely efforts will serve to effectively undo the spiritual damage caused by this present dark age, or that any wisdom we alone possess will help to light a pathway for us through the darkness of the Unseen world beyond the circles of this world, is a form of egocentric madness and empty pride all its own. The hubris of civilization is its ultimate origin.

It is a stance we have to learn to give up if we wish to become the kinds of people who can really and genuinely be open to the help that is out there, waiting for us, in the Unseen. We need allies. We cannot walk forward alone.

A lot of people, as I have indicated, reject this idea of our personal insufficiency very furiously. They claim that they don't think the problem is all that bad, and that they are "more happy than not." And I always tell them that it's perfectly understandable why they can feel happy to the degree they claim; at the heart of each person is the *blissful power of life itself*. It's a very strong power; it doesn't take much to lure it out. Let your guard down just once, and it can spring out in many subtle ways.

Deep down, no matter how miserable we might become, there's always this thing that feels like hope; there is always the idea, the possibility, that all will be well in the future. That's the Quick in us- and it might be all we really have to get by on, unless we're just born very lucky. Those who truly lose all connection to that feeling and the basic, life-driving optimism it engenders tend to rapidly die from one cause or another, most often suicide.

But even if a person could find a way to maintain that genuinely hopeful and happy feeling day and night, they would still find themselves very often doing things and feeling things that they'd truly rather *not* do or feel.

And sometimes- it's inevitable- we will hurt the people we love most, which is not something we'd ever want to do. Our feelings of compassion for others are shattered and ineffective because of this great helplessness we feel: the helplessness of being so completely tangled up in the malformed human social world. Those we love most, they, too, will let us down, in many ways. Political systems will, too.

We regret many things; we wish we had known so many things in hindsight, after it's far too late. We get deceived by others (when we should have known better) and despite our best efforts, the struggle against fear and uncertainty takes up a lot of our lives. Even if we're not consciously doing it, most of us are daily fighting a desperate and losing battle against fear, disillusionment and uncertainty. It emerges in our disquieted dreams, in our desperate seeking of more and more stimulation or euphoria, even in habitual self-harm and final self-destruction.

The mind is surprisingly resilient; it is brilliant at re-storying things to make even the worst situation more palatable, more bearable. We tell ourselves that many of the constant sorrows we endure simply exist because "that's just the way things have to be" or "it's just a normal part of life." We take the "tough and mature" stance- rejecting the sorts of things I am saying here by saying some variation of "*grow up, man- life's hard, but the point is to endure, adapt, and overcome those things! No one ever said it was supposed to be all easy!*"

While it's true that life will always have challenges and *always did* have challenges, the sheer amount of extraneous and artificial challenges we've come to normalize and accept as "*just the way things are*" is crazy, and we're simply wrong to assume it's all normal. Life as we encounter it at present is *not* naturally intended to be what it has become: so full of stress, angst, noise, hurry, moronity, and lostnesss. But we have these particular strands of denial we hold on to with great devotion, for the very understandable sake of our own sanity.

We take shelter in certain stories that maybe we shouldn't, stories intended to act as fallout shelters for the chronic hurting of our world and our lives. But the pain of the world, the *tears of the world* are too great. By "world", I *always* mean the *human social world*, not the "World" with a capital W- not the natural world, and not the spirit world.

One of the ways we interrupt or break this system of constant and clever denial is by *surrendering our egocentric desire to avoid admitting to weakness*. If we can do that, admit to how little we actually know about the deeper truths of ourselves and this world, and admit to our inability to do very much at all that will solve so much of this pain we have embraced, then *new possibilities open up for us*: new possibilities of mind and of the soul.

It is my sincere belief that the Master and many powers in the Unseen world all desire to shed clarity onto us and bring us to lasting peace. He and They want to restore us to a condition of deeper wisdom and far less pain. The "existential drift" that we have normalized is a *symptom of a disease*, not a simple, natural, and normal aspect of life.

The Ancestral powers want us spared from the madness. They have the power to help and they have the *motive* to help: they are part of our great chain of Ancestral relationship. We share the same life they manifest. The Great Fore-parents want to aid in our relief and wisdom-recovery. They do not want us being in the grip of all this insanity in such an unbalanced, unaware way as we have become.

But this insanity is a function of a darker Fateful weather-pattern that none of us, not even Them, chose to occur or become real. It's just a tide that comes in, from time to time. There's no need to seek to blame someone for it. Maybe "dark tides" like the one that besets us now have happened many times before. Whatever the case, we face our challenge with this one, right now. And we have more going for us, spiritually speaking, than we might realize.

Ancient attempts on the part of *Them over There* to reach us on a deeper level were made throughout civilized history, so that life wouldn't have to be so one-sided and painful, but most importantly, *so that death wouldn't have to be so uncertain and terrifying*. As a consequence of the soul-damage we've all suffered, death *is* uncertain and terrifying for most people, and the Ghost-Roads beyond, which used to lead to Ancestral homes and fire-circles, now stretch off into the mists of "we know not where."

For many of the dead, each of them carrying their own fears, angers, hatreds, limitations, and soul-wounds into the deep, the track-way into the beyond is an uncertain and confusing place. At times, the track may disappear entirely.

We have good hope that the Ancestrally-related Fetch-Follower that accompanies most of us through life *and* into death will act as a guide when we die; but the Mysteries come to us at this point, and with them comes an offer of more aid and of more extraordinary alliance. They come with offers for help in times of highest need or crisis, and we would be foolish devils indeed to not accept these ancient helping hands so readily offered.

We have allied powers in the Unseen who want to help us. Not all powers in the Unseen care about our well-being, but some do, to a high degree. Some powers, of course, are enjoying preying upon us, slurping up our life-force in these wounded times. These powers love tragedy-shows like ours that bleed so much life-force. Other powers are indifferent. The powers who actually care, care because *we're part of their great extended family*. We have ancient bonds that we've long ago discarded into forgetfulness under the intoxicating power of breath and the amnesia-inducing power of civilized storytelling.

So, the Master reaches out and does this very important thing...

VIII: The Mystery of Allegiance to the Master and "All-Inbetween."

The Master's chief mystery is a mystery of *trust*. For those who will seek out a relationship with Him, and who will choose to trust Him *completely* to illuminate their paths through this world and into the condition beyond death, *all will be well*. This is the simple and liberating truth.

It sounds, to our civilized ears, "too easy" and "too good to be true." But this very theme of surrender into a trusting, simple, intimate relationship with the Lord of Infinite Light who is also the Lord of Infinite Life, who will then (as a consequence of that perfect trust) carry that trusting person into a condition of not only spiritual protection in life but into *freedom and bliss in death*, appears historically not only in ancient Greece, but in various places in India and in central Asia, and all the way to East Asia.

This theme- *Trust*- is the heart of the more "masculine" of the two mysteries I wish to discuss now.

An entity as powerful as the Master, who is as concerned   as He is with the dissemination of wisdom and with maintaining the healthy boundaries of this world, has few limits to how he can help people who open the doorway of relationship to him.

If anyone comes aside and really asks the Master for his help, and *if* that person chooses to lay aside the harmful echoes of the breathy ego (which always believes it is more capable of solving its own problems than it really is) *and further*, if that person will surrender to the Master's power and aid in realization and acceptance that they cannot, through any mortal power they *alone* possess, find their way through the spirit world or through death or the unseen, and cannot obtain the deepest wisdom on their own, then the Master-ordinarily acting through the agency of the spirits bound to him, will *seize* that person. He will seize them first in this life with his presence and protection, his hidden light from within and with the protection of those same serving spirits, and *then* he will seize them in death, to ensure their easy and successful guidance through that dark and obscure experience.

He will carry them through the darkness to his *Forest of Delights*, and establish them there in such a manner that they can *never* fall away from that happy spiritual condition or be lost from it by any woeful sling-stone or arrow-shot of dark Fate. There, in the *Hobb-Den Forest*, those fortunate people will *learn* and become wise and deathless like Him and his Hobbs.

The Master has chosen, by "seeing in every direction", to absorb the evils of the world onto himself and thus free us from the consequences of those evils *if* we ask him to help us. This will be so if we reach out to him, and give up on our egoistic attempts to think we can alone figure out the secrets of the whole world and what "good", "evil", and "wisdom" really are for ourselves.

Wisdom, it has been said, truly lies in knowing how little power we have to grasp what wisdom really is, or perhaps even what "good" and "evil" are. We are cursed by the pervasive cloud of the human social world's unwisdom, and we are in chains because of it: the chains of hate, of greed, of stupidity- they have damaged us all, even if we are individually great people who are gentle and helpful to others in our daily lives. We can always, through our genuine efforts, have *some* very authentic wisdom born in us. We can enjoy real and potent tastes of clarity, but we always run into severe limits for what it can do for us or for others. The joy we gain from the morsels of wisdom we find or attain is always under threat as we come to feel the limits imposed upon wisdom by the human social world.

No matter how deep we become as people, the masses of others around us cannot meet us to any extent deeper than they have met themselves- and this is one of the hardest truths of our modern interactions.

The civilized stories that proliferate around us create end-less walls for wisdom, and seldom a bridge or channel for it. We are instead inundated with myths of "progress" and "achievement." It's a civilized story, a civilized myth, that our purpose as humans is to explain everything, to know everything, to be capable of anything, to have total control over our emotions and feelings, and to ultimately be more powerful than nature.

That was never the point of any life. The deeper soul doesn't want or need that. We have to lay the allure of that aside, and then, in true rejection of those things, *we will learn* from the Other Powers, from the Deeper Powers, what we most need to know. The "Devil"- the Master- embodies all "evil" because he takes all the evil of the human world onto himself. He absorbs it, and when you absorb many things- as when you mix all colors if paint together in one bowl- you turn black, eventually.

All the insanity of our human world, it has a dark presence. He bears it all in and on himself as a protective act, and a purifying act. The use of "black" and "dark" here must be considered very distant and apart from any racial overtones or racial propaganda. "Black" and "dark" here simply refer to the Master being full of the hard consequences of so much unwisdom, violence, and sadness in the world. It is a poetic darkness completely divorced from any racial politics.

As World Indweller, he is the world's *Ward*, the protector of natural boundaries and the natural order. The crimes of human civilization have exceeded many boundaries for ages on end, and are now beginning to legitimately threaten the entirety of the natural world, too. The Master, as a guardian of the world-integrity, might have had no choice but to step up and become the dark terror that he now appears as from time to time. His primal power was always potentially frightening or awe-inspiring; now it is even more so.

Promising all of yourself to the Master- pledging to him "*All-Inbetween the crown of the Head and the soles of the Feet*" (such is the traditional formula)- means giving *up to him* completely, and becoming his pupil, his apprentice, his acolyte. The soul's destiny is changed forever by the Master's power after this act. That destiny, no *matter what*, will be one free of pain and in the glory of His boundless life and light after death, where the soul will learn. And that soul will become one of the deathless ones, in time. This trust for the Master assures that there is no evil in death for those who belong to him.

Anyone can do this, enter into this relationship, just as they are right now. A person doesn't have to be "good", and it really doesn't matter how "bad" they were before, so long as they are willing to accept the Unseen's great presence and strive to be as non-selfish and fair as they may for the rest of their days. It doesn't matter how smart a person is; the powers we're talking about trusting are far beyond human intellect. And it doesn't matter how young or old a person is; the Master Spirit takes all who will "come aside" and yearn to be free of the stories of civilization and the deceptions of the unrestrained, pain-mad ego. Because what we really are, and what really makes the world what it is, is far, far beyond anything we can comprehend.

So, unwisdom never need harm us or make us lost if we trust in the Master's wisdom utterly and completely. We can, as the ancient initiates did, live in better hope and die in perfect hope that *so long as we completely trust His guidance*, He will receive us. It will be so. In the grave, the line between mortal and immortal fades; There is a "crack" that opens up, that some souls can slip through.   If you are one of the Master's own, pledged to Him in perfect trust, He will take you right then. He will take you If *your soul does not resist in confusion or fear*- which it will not if you prepare yourself for death by creating a relational attitude of total trust for him throughout the life you have left.

He can make up for any doubts you might still harbor, for doubting the Unseen is a function of the unwisdom of our world. Even when we know better, we might still doubt many things that should not be doubted. The Unseen powers know that we can't help this at times, and the Master's power is more than enough to overcome the impact of doubt on you, so long as you will always make the effort at total trust. The most powerful living being's light or presence is omnipresent and available to all. His duly-bound servitor entities will come for you and guide you through and over death, and into the "Devil's Forest"- into the Piper's Meadow of Fayerie-bliss, the "*Green Field*" or the "*Green Meadow*" which is the very ongoing presence, in the Unseen World, of the now-vanished untainted lands that existed in our world long ago.

It is the ghost and soul of the world *as it was*, the "*pure world*" as it came from the Womb of the Mother, before the Ravenous Tide stained it red with blood and black with the soot of industry.

This *Undying Lands* or *Deathless Lands* notion is a localized form of the mystery of the "Shamanic Golden Age", the state that shamans in many primal cultures report experiencing when they journey into the Unseen World. They attain to the condition of the now-mythical *Foretime* when man and beast and spirits were united, and all could speak to one another with ease. It is a "time" and condition of freedom and power that still exists in the deep, in the core of reality, the true "Fayerie Land" wherein time is meaningless and ordinary divisions between beings fall away with ease.

If we wish to seek shelter in this special kind of relationship to the Master, the relationship that creates the situation in which we are taken into His fold in death and transformed into truly free beings (who then haunt this world, working no doubt on whatever mysterious things these entities get on about) there can be no hint of us trying to force another story onto any of this, any story of ourselves being "not that lost" or somehow "truly happy"- no one inside of civilization's wide prison-yard, in this disconnected and banal social world, can boast of knowing what lasting happiness feels like.

We might be lucky to find a lot of happiness (relatively speaking) and as children or young people perhaps, we might be fortunate to receive the gift of a temporary taste or a few tastes of real carefree joy. But the vast majority of our happiness in most of our lives will *always* be conditional and brief, and always vulnerable in many other ways to the heartless, unwise machinations of our societies and to the predatory behavior of the wounded people that surround us. We always live in a little fear of the simplest and most natural things we cherish being lost, alongside our lives being lost at the hands of the insane.

Witches went to the noose and pyre happy, as it was reported, knowing that soon they would be with the Master and in the strange, glorious invisible light of his presence, alongside the Fayerie-hosts. At the Sabbat, *when they met Him directly*, He gave them a taste of what freedom and bliss really felt like, and they knew they'd be in that condition soon.

The 16th century mass murderer/witch hunter Pierre De Lancre was told by a witch that "*The Sabbat was the true paradise*, where there was more joy than could be ex-pressed." Those who went there found time too short because of the pleasure and happiness they enjoyed. A 28-year-old female witch told him "The joy which they (the witches) had at the Sabbat *was but the prelude of a much greater glory.*"

Our many modern copies of happiness can be very great, but I feel that so many layers of circumstance and wickedness beset them that if we were hit by a dose of true and unhindered happiness, our bodily frames might burn away in a fire of unbearable delight. Real freedom and happiness is a wild and alien thing, glimpsed like a mystery-vision once you shatter or just crack civilization's "glass darkly." Real freedom is unlike anything that people who are heavily-invested in the civilized paradigm can comprehend.

What we truly are, as wandering souls having these hard experiences, are *wild and alien things* straining to return to the wild heart of the world's pure and surreal depths. Though that place is called "Hell" in a pejorative way now, it maintains both a mystique and a sacredness that we need, and it also contains the things that can heal us the most.

The idea of the "Expulsion from Eden" or the *fall from grace* is a civilized attempt to put words on a dim memory of the times before the Ravenous Tide, or before the shift that created a whole new world-order for human beings and made us normalize violent, insane things. It wasn't a "fall of man" at the beginning of time; this event was more recent than anyone could ever have imagined. Sometimes, civilizations try to conceptualize this "fall" as a fall of souls from a perfect heaven, into a suffering "lower world" of matter and darkness.

That, too, is false. That's a very flawed attempt to capture a truth that is based on something a bit more recent and simple, but whose terrible metaphysical pain has stung us so terribly that we can't help but picture it- and depict it- as a truly alarming cosmological matter.

Our deep existential pain makes us attempt to describe "what went wrong" not only in terms of self-blame, but in terms of epic (and quite over-ripe, in my opinion) cosmological stories that are centered around vast human disobedience. They are soap-operas of cosmic horror and failure, and (naturally enough) centered on ourselves and our destinies as humans as though we are the most special aspects of all nature.

All of these efforts are colored by lack of wisdom. Not just humans, but countless other beings have suffered from the terrors of the Red Wave.

If one can identify with the Master, or one of his duly bound serving daimons in this life, one changes how they die and how they live. Formal rituals of identification with him and with the Hobb-men were many in the past: they were the very heart of the ancient mysteries of Dionysos, for example. Dionysos must be considered one of the primary historical Pagan cults that were essentially direct channels to the pure "Religion of the Master", for Dionysos, as the God of *Zoë,* was the God of Boundless Life-Force, of *Indestructible Life-* the very divine person associated with the primordial power of life.

Associated with Dionysos is practically every iconic symbol

and form known for the Master in later lore, from serpents to bulls to deer and goats, as well as the presence of blood-rites, satyr-daimons, frenzied, entranced men and women (and sorcerers) having supernatural rave parties in the name of Dionysos outside of the walls of cities and outside of the boundaries of civilization. Dionysos, like the Master, also has many, many names and different shapes and forms. Above all, his mysteries promised *freedom in life and in death*.

In the mysteries of Dionysos, as Carl Kerenyi has exhaustively recorded and revealed, was the belief that at the time of death, men and women who had ritually identified with Dionysos and his band of reveling, wild, and sacred entities in this life *would be met by them, and guided by them away from this life and into an erotic experience of the God himself*-and through a sexual encounter with him or one of his entities, be transformed into deathless beings, dwelling in the eternal bliss of the God forever and existing as timeless/deathless bacchante-satyrs and maenads. The parallels with the Witch's sexual intercourse with the Devil, or the man or woman's sexual congress with the Fetch-bride or Fetch-mate, are perfect parallels.

In this, I believe, is one of the prime origins of the somewhat declined or degenerated "mystery cult" belief-relics that some Witch-cults in the past still maintained possession of, in southern as well as northern Europe. My full analysis of the Mysteries of the Sabbat are outside of the scope of this work, but suffice it to say, more than a few of the folkloric icons surrounding the complex of the S*pirit-Flight Sabbat*, and the intimate relationships between human and Fayeries/ humans and demons, would indicate the presence of a symbolic language discussing and pointing the way to soul-transformation, both in life, and in death, in the Master's name.

If a person can accept what I say about our radical human insufficiency (on account of our *civilized lostness*) with respect to finding wisdom, or with respect to ever hoping to find "the good path" through the Unseen after death, that person can actualize the most essential and basic form of the Master's mystery of guidance and relationship by going to some lonely place at some good time, like a sunset or a sunrise or a moonrise, and turning their mind and soul fully to the Ancient One, and then saying with their audible voice the following line ten times: **"Lord of Infinite Life, Lord of Infinite Light, I give you adoration and take shelter in you."**

You must really believe that *He can hear your words*, because He can, right in the ground or land wherever you're standing. You must say these words with *full intention* of trusting Him completely with the full guidance of your soul's pathway beyond this life when you die. You must *trust that* He will take you away at the moment of your death- no matter when or how you die- and establish you in his Hidden Kingdom.

If you can do that, it will be so, no matter what. No matter what other pains or troubles or obscurities might invade upon your life, it will be so. If you create this relationship of complete trust with the Master, he will absorb the evils that beset you, and you will be taken in death to the Green Field where real wisdom will be yours to learn. At some point after that, you will obtain the metamorphosis into the deathless condition. You must believe that such a potent entity as the

Master is truly powerful enough to accomplish this- for He is.

The extent of your trust transforms how your soul will receive the darkness and the light of death. Your trust creates a relationship all on its own, and the Master, forever the Secret Father of humankind, will receive you. He has extended an invitation many times already. No living person has anything at all to lose in seeking this simple communion and this transformation through trust.

When you consider the reality of this easy practice, you see that it is, at the simplest level, the *ultimate religious act of trust in the integrity of the Universe.* You are in essence entrusting yourself to the heart of the boundless lifeforce that exists in all things, and the Great Person who mediates so much of it to your human condition. It is a simple act of doing as the Wind Indweller bade the Inuit people do when he told them "*Be not afraid of the universe.*"

Those who attain to the Master's Presence and to his Forest, that realm which is his boundless presence manifest as an arboreal landscape of beauty and peopled by those spirits bound to him for various reasons, *do not lose the memories gained in life when they were in possession of the breath soul.* I believe (based on my own research and extraordinary inquiries) that this condition allows for recall of many other experiences had under different breath souls as well, or in many other shapes a person's wandering soul may have lived in.

I've always wondered if the "*fair and lovely realm*" of the Horned God that Gerald Gardner taught his initiates about, and in which some believed they would all meet again, wasn't a rendition of this same idea. The notion of memory being preserved beyond death and people remembering the "limbs" of previous lives or existences seems to ring from the Wiccan adage "*and ye shall meet, and know, and remember, and love them again.*"

Other practices, ritual performances, and extraordinary encounters can be sought to bring about the identification with the Master that might win a person safe passage through the obscurities and confusions of this life and beyond. I encourage them. but this simplest practice of "giving adoration" and *taking refuge* in his guidance is by far the most powerful practice of all, in my estimation, due to its sheer simplicity and deep intimacy.

It is a foremost and best practice, due to how it takes *our own self-focus out of the equation* and allows us to completely trust the power of the *Sacred Other*. Our human limitations won't become deadly foes or unwise nooses for our desperate necks *if the chief causal force acting on us*, with regards to our future path or destiny, isn't primarily a matter of whatever personal power we have obtained or what limitations we personally bear.

Our every road in this world, for the rest of this life, transforms under the influence of the mighty and simple trust. Every road and every experience we have becomes a "triumphal procession" towards our destiny of wild freedom and joy with the most free beings in this cosmos, which will be just a few short human years (in the larger scheme of things) away. There will be no more wandering lost ever again, beyond the boundaries of this life, and all of that because of the Master's guidance. It is a guidance he can easily give and *will* give if we open ourselves in trust to it. For He is, as the old Scottish saying has it, "*Always Good to His Own.*"

IX: The Mystery of the Red Bread and the Red Drink

The more "feminine" branch of the Mysteries, at least in the terms I understand them, is associated with the Person of the Earth Indweller in her hypostasis as the Fayerie Queen. It is focused around the ritual and sacramental consumption of a special bread and drink- the *Sacrament of Bread and Wine* which transforms a human being's body and soul in life, and thereby transforms their destiny in death.

This *Red Meal*, as we have come to refer to it, is not related in any significant manner to the Christian "Eucharist" rite. It is a re-enactment, in symbolic form, of the sexual intercourse that Thomas Rhymer- a historical human being- had with the Queen of *Elfland*, identified as the Underworld in the ballad bearing his name. Whether she was the Earth Indweller herself, or one of her serving-women, one of the female spirits of her company makes no difference. Sexual congress with her, as a representative of the Underworld and the deepest transforming and regenerative root- powers of Nature and this world, was enough to have the "Underworld Initiation" mediated to Thomas Rhymer and to transform his body and soul, winning for him a new life and a new destiny.

The ritual of the Bread and Wine itself is revealed in full in the special language of the Ballad of Thomas Rhymer, which is found in the invaluable Child Ballads collection. And the effect of the ritual, its impact on Thomas, is also described in full detail. A full treatment of this ritual and its mysteries is given by me in the second portion of this book, in the three essays you will find there: "The Secret Heart of the Origin Tradition", "The Lore of the Elfhame Cross", and my own arrangement of the Ballad of Thomas Rhymer. All that is required to actualize this particular transformation-mystery is there.

The Ballad of Thomas Rhymer answers one of the perennial questions about our modern life: why are we disconnected, in such a thorough-seeming way, from the Unseen world? The answer lies in the *River of Water* and the *River of Blood* that separates our two worlds, which Thomas encounters in the Ballad as the Queen of Elfhame and he attempt to cross into the Underworld. Thomas, riding on the horse of the Fayerie Queen, has to wait 40 days while they wade across both rivers, to reach their otherworldly destination.

These two wide, fluid barriers are formed of all the tears shed on earth above, and all the blood that is shed on earth above. In other words, the extreme suffering, violence, and injustice of the human world- the great grief of the world- *is the factor that has separated us from the Netherworld and its regenerating, wisdom-granting potencies*. No larger indictment of the civilized or modern world-order has ever been recorded in folkloric tradition than this.

Any who take the sacrament of Bread and Wine in this life will have a transformed destiny in death. Their soul, when it travels to the Crossroads *in* the Underworld, will not face the impossible choice of taking either the left road or the right road, neither of which leads to the place of the highest attainment of wisdom and freedom. *They will have a third choice made available to them*, due to the transformation the meal and drink bestows upon them. The bread and wine are symbolic of the "blood and seed"- the sexual and life-bearing fluids- and of sexual intercourse with the initiatrix.

That contact, whether in symbolic form through the bread and wine in our world, or accomplished directly in the Unseen, transforms the wandering soul of the partaker. For it is said, and remains forever true: "*What is done symbolically in this world is done in actuality in the Unseen.*"

The Earth Indweller was responsible for the establishment of many mysteries in the ancient world, including the most famous of all mysteries from the time of civilization: The Eleusinian Mysteries. The Mystery-Rite of the Red Meal is an accomplishment of precisely what those mysteries promised, as well as what the Allegiance-mysteries of the Master promise: *life with better hope, and death with a better hope for a better destination*. Those who gain access to the "Third Road" that leads into Fayerie-Elfhame, and thus access to the Green Field of the Mother, find themselves in a place where they are transformed and granted *Justification*: lasting spiritual freedom and near-omniscience, along with the *Tongue that Cannot Lie* (the power of prophecy.) This is all sprung from seeing the past and the future come together as one in the Great Below.

They become the "Master Men" and "Master Women" or "Gray Women" of folklore- Justified humans who have attained not just the state of re-capturing the original, spontaneous freedom of life, but also a further transformation into another class of entity, for all time or eternity. This location in the Underworld, this fair, good meadow or green field is also "*The Field of the Goat*", the *very same location* that those who trust in the Master and have the relationship of true allegiance to him are carried to. They are the same place.

Those who are initiated by the sacred meal into the "Third Road Mystery" can trust completely that they will obtain to that happy condition after this life ends. Those who are initiated by the formation of the sacred trust relationship to the Master can also fully believe that they will attain to that condition; in fact, the assurance that they *will* depends, to an extent, on their simple and honest trust.

Anyone who is "initiated" into both branches of these mysteries can rest assured that whatever quality of mind or soul is dominant in them in death will be *received* and act only as a friend- never a foe, never a distraction or a blockage during the death-transition. Dull states of mind will be enlivened; poisonous ones will be soothed.

In a sense, taking both initiations is the ultimate recovery of wholeness, the *covering of all bases* esoterically considered. This is because the Trust Mysteries are surely more a matter of the intellect and therefore the Breath Soul (though they impact all of the souls) and the Bread and Wine mysteries are more a matter of the wandering or free soul (though they impact the intellect in life, too.) To satisfy both souls is to assure together what either of the mystery-understandings and experiences would have assured individually: the best possible condition being attained to when the light of this life has set.

But there are countless other benefits before death, too, for any legitimate initiate or person who has obtained these subtle or coarse transformations. There are many potential

forms or power, insight, extra-normal vision or sensory power an initiate might acquire. There is a sense of courage and peace that can appear; there may be blessings of luck, and there is an ongoing sense of wonder, a subtle feeling of *connection with the extraordinary* which cannot be described, only experienced.

PART TWO

THE MYSTERY-CULT OF THE ELFHAME CROSS

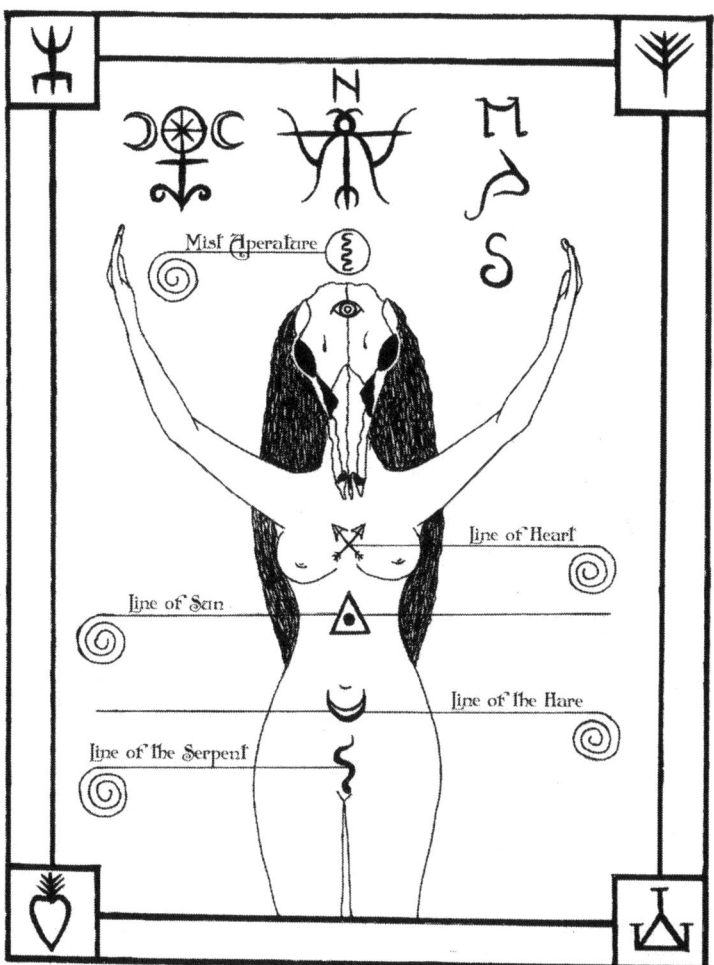

Mist Aperature

Line of Heart

Line of Sun

Line of the Hare

Line of the Serpent

Earth Indweller: The Land

Generosity Pours Forth from Below

Great Grandmother of Souls, who dwells at the heart of the darkness below, you are the beginning and the end of our wandering stories, and of all stories. If our every step in this world does not move us one step closer to you, then our steps are taking us nowhere. When the sun of this life has set, this soul you have birthed alone remains luminous.

Elfhame's green meadows are the native country of these souls. You are the joy of wandering souls. You are the truth that wandering souls celebrate, but are hindered in expressing above, because of the unwisdom of the world. You are the lasting one, forever supporting every foot that presses upon the Earth. Whatever is whispered or said into the space left when a clod is cut from the ground echoes in your ear; it enters into your timeless trance.

Things buried below the ground with reverence appear at the foot of your throne, and there, the gentry of Elfhame receive them. So, Boundless Life Mother, receive us when our hours have caught us, and the earth opens to take our remains.

Not to the right will we go, nor to the left, but because we have eaten the Red Bread and drunk the Red Drink, because we have received of you the nameless blessing that changes the bones of the soul, we will go a third way, beyond the Elphillock and into the Green Field where wisdom blossoms without effort. There, we will be Justified. We will have the tongue that cannot lie. We will know the virtues of all growing things. We will be kilted and draped in green, and live beyond life and death forever.

The Ballad of Thomas Rhymer

Arranged by Robin Artisson
Drawing upon source Child ballads 37A, 37B, and 37C

* * *

TRUE THOMAS lay over on yon grassy bank,
And he saw a Lady of beauty profound,
A Lady that was brisk and bold,
Come a-riding over the ferny mound.

Her skirt was of the grass-green silk,
Her mantle of velvet most fine,
And all along her horse's mane
Hung fifty silver bells and nine.

True Thomas he took off his hat,
And bowed low down to his knee:
"Well met thee, my Lady most fair,
For you are the true flower of this country."

"O no, O no, Thomas," She says,
O no, O no, that can never be,
For I'm but a Lady of the Unseen Land,
Come out a-hunting, as you now see.

"Harp and carp, Thomas," She said,
"Harp and carp along with me,
And if you dare to kiss my lips,
Surely of your body I will be."

"Betide me weal, betide me woe,
That weird shall never frighten me!"
Soon he has kissed her rosy lips,
All underneath the Eildon Tree.

"But you must go with me now, Thomas,
True Thomas, you must go with me,
For you must serve me seven years,
Through weal or woe as chance may be."

She turned about her milk-white steed,
And took True Thomas up behind,
And always when her bridle rang,
The steed flew swifter than the wind.

For forty days and forty nights
They wade through red blood to the knee,
And he saw neither sun nor moon,
But heard the roaring of the sea.

For it was a mirky night, without light,
As they waded that blood to the knee;
For all the blood that's shed on earth
Runs through the springs of that country.

O they rode on, and further on,
Until they came to a garden green:
"Light down, light down, you Lady free,
Some of that fruit let me pull for thee."

"O no, O no, True Thomas," She says,
"That fruit must not be touched by thee,
For all the plagues that are in hell
Light on the fruit of this country."

"Hold your hand, Thomas," She says,
"Hold your hand, that must not be;
It was that cursed fruit of thine
That beggared man and woman in your country."

"But I have a loaf here in my lap,
Likewise a bottle of sweetest wine,
And before we go much farther on,
We'll rest a while, and you may dine."

When he had eaten and drunk his fill,
"Lay your head upon my knee,"
The Lady said, "before we climb yon hill,
I will show you wonders three."

"O do you see yon narrow road,
Thick beset with thorn and brier?
That is the path of righteousness,
Though after it few inquire."

"And do you see that broad, broad road,
That lies across yon lily'd leven?
That is the path of wickedness,
Though some call it the road to heaven."

"And do you see that bonny road,
Which winds about the ferny hill just so?
That is the road to Fair Elfland,
Where you and I this night must go."

"But, Thomas, you must hold your tongue,
Whatever you may hear or see,
For, if you speak a word in Elflyn land,
You'll never get back to your own country."

He has gotten a coat of the even cloth,
And a pair of shoes of velvet green,
And till seven years were past and gone,
True Thomas on earth was never seen.

The Secret Heart of the Origin Tradition

The *Sacrament of Bread and Wine*- also called the **Red Meal**- is the ritual event wherein the genuine *Fayerie Faith* and the entire essence of true *Old Religion* emerges from a background of folklore, metaphysics, and sorcery and enters into the breathing immediacy of our lives. It is an opportunity to actualize a very potent mystery. No act more than the regular taking of the Red Meal- this feast that unites Seen and Unseen- embodies or "sums up" the way of the living mystery of the Underworld Initiation, or of *Provenance Traditionalism*, a name I give to the quest for hidden keys to transformation within folklore and myth. It likewise acts as the "spine" of the power-transfer and power-keeping activities of witch covenants, if they are wise.

Those who regularly engage in this act are parts of an authentic mystery religion ages old, as they directly participate in the inner life of a sacred message that certain key components of historical folklore and myth have won for us. Those who engage in it regularly- at least once a month or at minimum four times a year- can be guaranteed the friendship of certain forces in the Unseen world, and all that implies.

The Red Meal can be done not only for oneself or a small group of devoted, but for other-than-human powers that share our world: its blessing can be transmitted, verbally, the ritual done on behalf, of the spirits of places, or of beasts, who can benefit in the long term from it. The Red Meal is a *symbolic act*, recreating the main events of the Ballad of True

Thomas, reenacting the events of his initiation and transformation. But always remember- *whatever is done symbolically in our world is done in actuality in the Unseen.*

First I shall give the "script" of the ritual performance. The next essay to follow this one will exhaustively describe what all of the symbolism of both the ritual and the Ballad it is based upon means. Below the ritual script will be a description of all the ritual actions (such as pronunciation for strange words, or "saining signs" and the like.)

* * *

The Red Meal is performed by getting a cup (wood, silver, earthenware or glass) of red wine, ale, or cider, and a bowl or plate (wood, silver, or earthenware) of dark bread- wheat bread, rye bread, the darker and redder the better. You can use any bread if you can't get that.

You place them in a triangle made of twigs or branches, or in a triangle drawn with flour. Holding your hands over them in a "triangled hand" form (hands completely flat, fingers all together but with thumbs protruding, palms facing down, tips of thumbs touching and tips of forefingers touching) one makes three taps or knocks on the ground or floor (you naturally do that before you "triangle" your hands) and say the following over the cup and bowl/plate:

I sain this bread and drink
In the name of the King of Elfhame.
The gift of the kingdom of death is life in abundance.
What was white became red,
So Master of Life and Death, make it white again:
Akramachamarei
Break the dark spell that binds this food

And let it serve the nourishment of my body and soul.

(Here you drawn the saining signs in the air above the cup and bowl or plate)

(three more knocks on the ground or table or floor as before, then return your hands to triangled)

I sain this bread and drink
In the name of the Queen of Fair Elfland,
For this is the nourishing increase of her body.
By your power, change the seed and blood Fair Queen:
Akramachamarei
Lift the plague that lights on the fruit of this country
And let me rest, and let me dine.

(Here the saining signs are again drawn in the air above the cup and bowl or plate)

At this point a sip is taken from the cup, savored and swallowed, and a piece of bread is eaten slowly. This "point of communion" is meant to be silent and meditative. All who are taking part in the meal share in it this way, one by one.

Before all others eat or drink, it must be announced "*This is not the bread and cup of heaven; this is the bread and cup of She who rules in the Great Below.*"

What remains in the cup and what remains of the bread is poured into another bowl together, and brought and left at the roots of a tree which is ideally very large or old and out of the way, or a natural body of water (pond, lake, river), a deep hole in the earth, a large rock that has a "cup" shaped indention on it, the side of a hill, brought to the edge of a well-blazing bonfire, or poured directly onto the earth of a field or meadow into a circle of nine small or fist-sized stones.

If no such places are available, you can put the remains in a wooden or earthenware bowl and put it next to a hearth or fireplace, or onto a shelf or shrine-space specifically set aside for the honor of the Old Powers, before removing it the next day to an out-of-the-way natural place to pour it out and allow it vanish naturally.

Wherever you end up "giving the rest over" to one of these places, you say:

True Blessings Be upon the People in the Hollow Earth
The Goodly Neighbors All;
True Blessings Be upon the Spirits in this Land;
And the Blessing of this Meal be upon me (or us)-
Joy to my body on Earth and my soul in the Meadows of
Elfhame.

(three taps or knocks here completes the rite.)

* * *

The "saining signs" are a hex-sign (three strokes of the finger, one being a straight line above the meal, and two more making an "X" across that line as though it were an axis for the X) followed by two equal-lines making an equal armed cross symbol right *on top of the hex sign*. It all ends up looking like an eight-pointed star has been drawn over the vessels.

This represents the triple crossroads in the Underworld that the Fayerie Queen carried Thomas Rhymer to, followed by the quadruple cross-roads of This World, or the four-directional outward world. *This is seen and unseen coming together*. Three and four together make seven- the uncanny number which (among other things) was the number of years many beings were "imprisoned" in the Unseen, or "away" before returning endowed with super-normal insights or initiatory transformations. It was also the amount of years Thomas spent in the Green Field of Elfhame, undergoing his transformation.

The word of power **Akramachamarei** is pronounced "uh-CROM-uh-com-er-ay" (the "com" in that sounds like the "com" in "dot com") and it literally means "*break the spell*"- it is an ancient word of banishing for bad powers or bad magic, but also an ancient name for the Master.

If you are doing this in your house, and you have a hearth or fireplace, you can add the following line to your "giving":

True Blessings Be upon the Dweller in this Hearth and those who live in this house.

If you are doing the Red Meal with the intention of gaining help or favors for yourself or someone else, for some need, you can add this portion to your giving:

A Blessing come upon x.
For whom this holy bread and drink is offered.
Powers in the Deep, aid him/her in x.-
Here we give something of the Red world
For something of the White.

* * *

It is very important to understand that this form of the Red Meal is the most transformatively potent, in that it converts the interior *red essence* of the bread and drink into their Otherworldly *or white form.* By eating them, a man or woman is creating a symbolic act of congress, communication, and interaction (one mythological version of which is sexual contact with Fayerie beings) with the Powers that transform souls in the Underworldly Metamorphosis.

This is the same contact that the before-mentioned Thomas Rhymer had with the Fayerie Queen, from which he gained his extraordinary powers. A brief review of the Ballad of Thomas Rhymer will reveal much insight into the form and function of this most potent of all Red Meals.

All "Red Meals" *are attempts to create a bond between we above the earth, and those below it-* this one is the most esoterically potent of all in the sense that it summons to presence and immediacy the interior dimensions of the hoped-for "Underworld Initiation" that the Fayerie-people legendarily bestowed upon a fortunate few in the past. The ordinary "red" bread and wine, when "unbound" by the Spell of the Saining, are released from the subtle but ominous spiritual and metaphysical poisons of the human world, and their giving as a gift *after that* to the Fayerie people transmits a mighty blessing even to them.

You may place, in the bread and wine saining words, the name by which you best know the King and Queen of Elfhame under. This will not fail to make the rite more powerful; the name I use for the Fayerie King (the Master) is a secret that is not for use outside of my Covenant, but it was won by me through an enormous amount of spiritual questing and extraordinary operations of (among other things) divination. Myth and folklore does not lack in potent names for the Master in his hypostasis as King Below, (or in any of his many forms) so a cunning person should search for those things very diligently. Without any special names at all, however, the Red Meal will function full well as it is written.

One of the most important names by which I know the Queen, however, is already released in some places, and I can say it here- *Laudine*. I only ask that you not repeat that name around to people without reason, and never use it disrespectfully or flippantly.

If you can make the bread for this meal yourself, bake it straight from scratch, all the better- it rises up from an already potent offering to an act of sublime mystical force. But any fresh bread will do- and the more peaceful and steady and simple you can be inside your own soul and mind while performing this ancient rite, the better it will be for you, and the subtle relationships it forges with the Unseen.

The Lore of the Elfhame Cross

The Elfhame Cross sigil or symbol given here is a *map of the Road to Elfhame* or the Underworld. It shows a crossroads at its top, but one that has the "Third Road" (the top-most line) shown or revealed- this is the secret road to the Green Field within Fayerie-Elfhame or the Queen of the Underworld's Meadow Unseen, where Thomas Rhymer "*that night went*" with her.

Starting from the bottom of the sigil and moving up, you have the road to the Underworld. It reaches the hedge- the metaphysical dividing point between Seen and Unseen, which in this case, is the presence of the "river(s) dividing"- the body of water being another primordial symbol for the dividing boundary between this world and the world beyond (*à la* the River Styx.) Here, where a strong line crosses the central stem of the image, are the two rivers- one of water, and the other of blood- or, as some might have it, a single river of water and blood- that Thomas had to spend a very long time crossing (forty days and nights), from the back of the Fayerie Queen's horse.

This represents all of the tears of woe shed in our world, which end up in the depths; the tears of the living "soak the ground" and become this river of woe, which not only divides the living from the dead (the dead don't weep) but acts, in some manner, as a *psychic barrier of trauma* that can break connections between the two worlds. The river of blood, on the other hand, is all the blood that is shed in our world, in violence, again, soaked into the ground and becoming this potent dividing force.

Continuing up the symbol, after crossing the river/rivers, you reach the Crossroads- which, when Thomas first arrives, is *not* three ways, but *two*: a right and left path. The *Crossroads of the Underworld*, the older form of any crossroads, is *not* a "four way" crossroads, but a *three way*- a road that forks.

The ancient tradition tells us that a special tree grows here, where the ways diverge- the Tree of Life. Its fruits are dangerous, however- the many ancient admonitions to avoid eating the fruits of the Underworld extend from a true place of wisdom. Upon the fruits of that tree "alight the plagues of the world above"- meaning that until we are transformed (and thus, until the tree is transformed) our bodies are essentially given to death; the fruits of our bodily life are mortal, and prone to death.

The pain of the above-world, all its tears and blood, settle down upon the below like an insidious dew falling from above. In the same manner that these hardships infect us in our daily lives, they infect the subtle world in ways, or at least our experience of it. The soul receives some of the woeful impact of the traumas of life. The forces of life in us and in our food are not only prone to death, but laced with a kind of metaphysical toxin born from the sheer amount of pain and injustice working its way through the human social world.

There is another interpretation here, which should be considered parallel to the standard "Tree of Life" interpretation. There is not only a tree at the crossroads, but a garden- and since the ballad never identifies from where Thomas seeks to gain the "fruit" for the Queen, it may be that he was attempting to pluck a fruit not from the true, but from another plant.

In ordinary interpretations, it would seem to be a no- brainer that the "fruit upon which all the plagues of hell alight", the fruit that the Queen claims "beggared the men and women" in the human world, is not only a fruit from the tree, but a reference to an apple, or the forbidden fruit of Eden. But it is *possible* that a deeper layer is present here, and that the Queen (and a darker voice from inside the depths of the tradition) is referring to *grain*, which is the fruit of a grass, and the essence of agriculture, which birthed human civilization and led to the many woes and "beggaring" of the world.

I only mention this as a curious and subversive notion. I think the implication that Thomas was reaching for the fruit from the Tree of Life is plain, but I can never resist mentioning this grain possibility.

The left fork leading away from the crossroads becomes the road "beset with thorns and briars"- it is the way of righteousness, though, not surprisingly, "after it, few inquire." The right fork becomes the "broad road" that goes across a pleasant field (the "lily leven")- that is, in the words of the Elf-Queen, the "path of wickedness", though "some call it the road to heaven."

The left fork represents a wilder road, all thorned and overgrown: the way non-human animals in our world naturally live. It is the path not only of those beings who live in such a manner as to not transgress nature's laws, but also the path of righteous human beings or other entities that choose to sacrifice themselves in various ways for the betterment of all.

The right fork represents the "broad road"- that wide and easy way that nearly all human beings follow, whether they realize it or not- the way of the vast majority of humans. It represents the Fateful entanglements nearly all of us have with social forces, family ties, and the destinies of nations, institutionalized religions, and all the other (ultimately unimportant) social fictions that people consider to be the most important things imaginable. This is the *road of wickedness* because it is the path of least resistance, with regards to the hidden (and sometimes not so hidden) moral dimension of living: the path of what is easy, not what is right.

It is the road of tyrannical states, of megachurches, bloated corporate entities, huge herds of people gone collectively mad, of anonymity, of dullness and uncreative tedium. It is also the road of greed, of materialism, of living unwisely in the world regardless of how it impacts the world.

These two roads are the only two choices that most humans who make it this far ever get. When human beings die and their souls arrive at the metaphysical "point" of the Crossroads, nearly all take the "broad, broad" road and return, eventually, through compulsion and mindlessness, towards incarnation in the world above or some other condition.

A few- a very few- may take the left road of righteousness, if they have the previous necessary conditioning and wisdom to do so, and they eventually seek incarnation again not under compulsion but through *willed, altruistic consent.* They become the world-shaping or world-changing heroes or the exemplary good people, the "local heroes" (who all almost always come to a tragic or painful end in some horrific manner.) Their road is one of great suffering, though much good can come of it.

However, Thomas Rhymer- like all who follow the path of the mystery- has another destiny, a road that *does not go left or right*. Thanks to his eating of the Red Meal given to him by the Queen, and his sexual encounter with her (in which his mind, body, and soul is transformed) he is allowed to perceive or see the "Third Road"- the one in the center, which is ordinarily hidden.

It is the road which "winds around the ferny hill". It is the Road to Fair Elfland, the path to the kingdom inside the depths of the Land, wherein reign the Fayerie Queen and her

King, and where dwell the blessed dead who have been transformed in such a manner before death (or shortly after death) to allow them to find that third road.

The bread and wine, representing "seed and blood", represent fundamental forces of life, but also sexual fluids-semen, and the menstrual blood that symbolize fertility. The bread and wine that the Queen presents to Thomas in lieu of the meal he was trying to prepare for her are the symbolic body and blood of the Queen, and eating them (and the act of Thomas laying his head in her lap) are disguised references to a sexual act of union that he experienced with her.

Thomas, fresh from the mortal world, was in no fit condition to "give" what he wanted to give to the Queen, even though it was right and respectful to want to give her food, or prepare for her a meal. He had to *receive transformations from her,* before he could be made ready for a real relationship with her, and real spiritual growth and fulfillment. He wanted to be active, but he *needed* to be passive, he needed to receive. A person must never forget this and the importance of this when we approach the great powers following any road, mystery or otherwise.

Eating the Red Meal in ritual form, a potent act by which the bread and wine are transformed by having the "plague and dark spell" taken off of them by the Lordly powers of the interior world, is intended to re-recreate the substance of what the Queen offered to Thomas and allow us to integrate it into our own bodies. Such an act is intended to make the Third Road available to those who partake, when they journey to the depths either in this life (via techniques of trance) or after their physical deaths. It is a true sacramental re-creation of what Thomas encountered at this point, before the Third Road was revealed to him.

The Third Road leads to Fayerie-Elfhame. Those who dwell there do not cycle into incarnation in any other condition under dread or mindless compulsion, or anything of that sort. They merge with the powers represented by the "interior earth" realm, the twilit-realm or the Green Realm that contains the seeds of many gifts, powers, or insights- such as the power of prophecy, which Thomas obtained through his seven-year initiatory visit. The Fayerie Folk are merged directly with the dimension of the ground, the Land, and can be experienced through the Land. Unless they choose to cycle from that state, or are compelled to by *deeper forces* than the forces that create the ordinary compulsion in humans running their rat-race on the "broad way", they are essentially deathless.

It is clear that the "Middle Way" to that world, which is in-side of every other phenomenon, is gained by obtaining a wisdom that steers people clear of the "left and right" extremes, in mind and soul. Bbut more than just some intellectual/philosophical (breath soul) understanding of the "bonny middle road" has to impact them before it makes a new destiny available to them. The transforming force of the Ruling Powers of the Underworld has to reach them on some deeper level, too.

This sigil of the Elfhame Cross, then, shows the "Third Way", the Bonny Road to Fair Elfland. That makes this sigil have "six" terminals or line-ends: three at the top, and three at the bottom. That makes it a representation of the Venusian number six, which is a number of harmony and harmonious union between male and female or between perceived opposites (like this world and the other.) Thomas fulfilled this union in spiritual-aesthetic iconography by being sexually united to the Fayerie Queen.

A person who has not been "embraced" by their Fayerie-Bride, or Fetch Bride, (or Fayerie King or Fetch-husband) and thus has not undergone the transformation, would be symbolized by this Elfhame Cross *minus* the third road up top- you can see what the symbol would look like in your imagination without it. That is the symbol of Man or Woman before initiation, before the Fayerie Metamorphosis. It has five line-ends, the number of struggle, pain, revolution and death. That is an adequate summation of what those who lack the *Fayerie-Metamorphosis* must face in this life *and* in the difficulties of the journeys after, which terminate in a hard choice at the crossroads, neither of which seems too ideal.

If you look at this sigil with the "third road" missing, you will also see that it looks like a simple mawkin-form: a person, with two legs two arms, and a head, turned upside down. It is symbolic of the inverted, suffering or unwise person.

But the transformed have direct spiritual access to the Depths, to the Fayerie world or Elfhame. They have access to its guidance at the subtle level, and to its extraordinary resources after this life (and perhaps before, if they are cunning.)

Gazing at the sigil reminds the depths of the soul that there is a middle way between hard dualities and "either/or" dilemmas. The sign symbolizes the desire of the wise to find their way into the presence of the Queen and King of the Unseen World and to receive the needed initiations to free themselves from the strange compulsions of unwisdom.

To utilize this symbol of the Elfhame Cross for Red Meals, draw this symbol in flour or with peeled white branches, twigs, or pebbles on the ground before you, and put your offering bowl that will receive the remains of your bread and wine at the top of the "Third Road." This symbolizes your offering going to the Fayerie or Unseen Powers. Stepping over this symbol on the ground is a sign of *Going Forth*, a formal "beginning" for any attempt to journey into the Fayerie World, demonstrating in a symbolic way what you intend- to go down the Third Way. Wearing this sign in some form would also be very beneficial.

All of the dead, when they reach the underworld, are in the *fayerie* condition. That most wander for a while down one road or the other, and then move on into other incarnations within the cycle of their souls, does not change this. Those that follow the "Third Road" are Fayerie also, but of a different kind- they become the transformed *Maister-Men* and *Fayerie-Lady* beings of various stages of attainment or insight.

Afterword: The Guide of Souls

In my book *Letters from the Devil's Forest*, I wrote the following passage:

"Witchcraft, alongside the earliest forms of religion- beginning with Provenance animism and going forward to the countless varieties of polytheism- does not teach about a "salvific" spirit world. Such a thing does not exist. The Master Spirit is not some "I got your back" god that people pray to for every little thing, or to be saved from the consequences of living in this world."

This may seem rather contrary to the spirit and message of "The Secret History", but I felt the need to clarify why I do not think it to be so. I stand on every word I said in the quote I gave above: animism and polytheistic belief systems don't really ever run into notions of "salvation" as modern Westerners understand that term because they don't believe that the world is broken or in need of salvation. However, the term "salvific" can have other shades of meaning. One can rightly say that they were "saved" from a danger like a spirit that caused an illness in them, when an allied spirit drove it away, and they were healed, their life spared. The word "saved" doesn't have to reflect the larger moral meaning it has in religions like Christianity.

Just so, in the Secret History, I discuss the idea of sacred and total trust in the Master causing a special kind of relationship to form with him in which he and his own allies are allowed to guide a man or woman through dangerous or hard times- particularly in the post-death journey. The real dangers that can sometimes exist in the post-death state are, indeed, things that one can be "saved" from, in the same way a person might be saved from a malevolent spirit by a protective helper. This is all I mean by it.

Just so, the idea of praying to spirits- or even the Master- for "every little thing" is foreign to traditional belief systems, of the animistic or polytheistic variety. Historical and modern humans may pray to spirits, or communicate with them in one manner or another in many situations of need, but the idea of an all-powerful entity having command over *every minute detail of life* is not just foreign to traditional thinking (and to my own thinking) but absurd besides, for many reasons.

When I say that the Master has the kind of wisdom and power to spare people from the consequences of unwisdom, particularly in the death-journey, that is not the same as being spared from the consequences of living in this world, broadly considered. No amount of trust or bond with the Master will save your living and tangible body if you leap into a volcano. The consequences of unwisdom, the obscurities in the mind and soul, however, can be affected by wise and powerful beings that we might have relationships with. *How those obscurities or confusions might limit us can be changed by the might of other allied powers*. This is the message of "The Secret History."

So, when I have said, in the past, "The consequences of actions and events in this world cannot be stopped or altered by the Unseen world except in the rarest of cases", I again, remain firm in this conviction. Shooting yourself in the head (or being shot in the head) has consequences that are going to be severe, in all but the rarest of cases. These kinds of tangible consequences are not the focus of the deeper insights to be found in "The Secret History."

I also made the following statement in *Letters*:

"I hate to reduce the Master to just a teaching role, but 99% of the time, that's how witches in the past experienced him: as a supporter of sorcery, and a mysterious partner in the process of gaining spiritual alliances and coming to such strange insights that perhaps few other humans will ever understand them.

The rest of the time, the human experience of him was as the exuberant Spirit of Life, of the vitalizing breath, partying at the extratemporal "Sabbats" and interstices of life- including the "party" that occurs on the occasion of actual deaths, when a new union with his power becomes possible to the deceased, a new relationship with him and the rest of the world besides."

This passage should suffice to alleviate any other concerns. "The Secret History" is a unique work on my part precisely because, for the first time, I discuss the Master in another guise, beyond the Teacher or Tutelary Spirit guise. I discuss him in another role, a role of *Psychopomp*, or Guide of Souls- the kind of entity that we might seek a relationship with for extraordinary guidance through certain high- intensity times of transition- like the transitional situation "that occurs on the occasion of actual deaths, when a new union with his power becomes possible to the deceased." This is again, the special focus of "The Secret History."

APPENDIX

Breathing, Following, Wandering: An Ecology of the Soul

1. What is the Soul?

The soul is a living expression- one of many living expressions, for they come in countless forms- of the vitality of Nature herself.

Nature here can be conceptualized as a system, as *the* System, comprised of the innumerable living forces that exist all interacting, *and* the background from which these living forces can be said to emerge somehow, which they all rely upon somehow, and within whose boundless field they all interact. These definitions of soul and Nature are intended to be baseline, to be simple. The further exploration I make of the soul below will add nuance.

Primal peoples worldwide regularly conceive of human beings (and other living beings) not being in possession of or in relationship to only a single soul, but to several distinct powers which have each been called "soul" in their time, by others.

Historical examples of this "multiple soul" belief include the West African and Haitian Vodou-based belief in the two souls that belong to each person, as elucidated by Maya Deren; the ancient Norse/Scandinavian belief in the several souls present for each human life, as elucidated by Claude Lecouteaux (and others); the Lakota Sioux belief in the several soul-type entities that converge upon each human life as elucidated by James R. Walker (among others); the ancient Greek belief in the two or more souls that belonged to each living being, as elucidated by Jan Bremmer; the two- souls belief of the Buryat and Yakut Siberians as elucidated by Sarangerel Odigon (and others); and the Inuit belief in the "Two Souls", as elucidated by Daniel Merkur, whose celebrated work "Powers Which We Do Not Know" greatly informs my short work here. I chose Merkur's work as my main vehicle of giving language to these subtle concepts on account of how well he sums up the essence of all the others I have studied.

Basically put, the "multiple souls" or the "two souls" model posits that each person is a triad of communicating, relating powers- a *body* alongside two souls- a *breath soul*, and a *free soul* (also called a wandering soul.) These terms have become standard anthropological terms used in studies of primal anthropologies. Several of the above authors mentioned utilize these terms in their own studies.

I will commence now in describing the two-souls perspective. It will be important to quote Merkur here, before I begin.

"In all, Soul dualism is an ideological system, designed not to describe but to explain psychological phenomenon. It is a system of psychology that is based on phenomenological data of psychic experience and systematized through philosophical speculation."

2. What is the Breath Soul?

The Breath Soul, also called the Body Soul, the Wind Soul, the Vitalizing Soul, or the Name Soul, is the collection of vitalizing force that is present in a body via the mechanism of breath. It circulates in and out, connecting the breath of that body- the wind of that body- to the larger "Wind of the World"- the airy, surrounding, animating atmosphere of the earth, and through that participation in the Great Air or the Great Wind, to all other breathing entities. The most in-depth analysis of the breath soul as it was experienced and understood by the ancient Greeks, the ancient Hebrews, and the Navajo people was done by David Abram in his excellent work "The Spell of the Sensuous."

A person obtains the breath soul at birth, when they commence breathing. The breath soul remains throughout the life, vitalizing the body, and the loss of it at any time means a rapid death. At death, the breath soul is expelled, breathed out for a final time, and lost. Within a short amount of time, it "depersonalizes"- it no longer belongs to the animate entity that had it during a life. It becomes indistinguishable from the greater Wind of the world, from whence it originally came. During life, the surface level "mind" or coarse consciousness operating through the body is connected to, and made possible by the breath. It is also connected to the most vital expressions of will, aggression, and self-assertion.

Merkur writes:

"The breath soul is responsible for life, warmth, and breath of the living body. Its loss is a direct cause of death. Insofar as it has a shape, it is said by the Chugach, Bering Strait, and Point Hope Inuit to be always anthropomorphic, regardless of species... In human beings, the breath-soul commences life lacking in experience, wisdom, or strength, for which reason "mind" constitutes a second component within it. It is best not to treat the mind as a separate type of soul, because the term used in many Inuit cultures for "mind" is the same as "name"... the implicit idea is that the breath-soul, which has developed "mind", becomes the name-soul after death and then functions as a guardian of succeeding generations."

Obviously, I just mentioned the perspective that the breath soul does not survive death in this way, to become a guardian spirit attached to a name it developed during life. Merkur points out that this belief appears to be unique to the Inuit. He writes:

"The idea of a postmortem breath-soul (i.e. name soul) is entirely specific to Inuit cultures. Although the Inuit would not so explain the strength derived from a guardian name-soul, the idea of solidarity with the deceased draws on the strength derived from social reinforcement in order to work its benefits."

The breath soul (like the body and the free soul) is part of a ceaselessly communicating system of life. The breath soul's chief method of communication is through sound- the sounds that animals and humans make, or the words of human language, are the breath *intensified*, the breath of the body turned into sound. The breath soul makes the most obvious example, in its every inhalation and exhalation, of vital participation with the living world.

A universal figure emerges inside of Inuit myth: The Person who Indwells the phenomenon of sky, air, weather and wind, whom the Inuit call *Sila*. This "Wind Indweller" is the source of breath souls, and through the connection of the breath soul (and the wind) to sound and noise, he is the teacher of not just language, but of sorcerous or magical words to shamans. He is the guardian of the world, of natural laws, and the avenger of broken taboos. The relationships of humans to the Indweller in the Wind is obviously profound and important; in that relationship the Inuit see each person's connection to the World itself, their ability to have peace in it, to live in harmony with all the other natural forces and laws. But as Merkur points out:

"To characterize Sila as the supreme being is inaccurate. In the animals, as in humankind, Sila's domain extends to the breath-soul; free souls are creations of the three great goddesses of the Inuit- the Earth Indweller, the Caribou Mother, and the Sea Mother. Sila might perhaps be described as the supreme being of the physical universe, but the Inuit also conceive of other realms of existence."

3. What is the Free Soul?

The Free Soul, also called the Wandering Soul, the Water Soul, or the Dreaming Soul, is the soul that pre-existed the body and the obtaining of the breath soul. It is often depicted as emerging from the "depths" of the world, from the Underworld or a Netherworld.

That the Earth Indweller (the Earth and Underworld Mother) is believed to be the source of free souls automatically positions the free soul as taking some kind of "birth" inside the earth, and emerging from its depths. The "waters below" or the watery abyss that has been conceptualized mythically as the Underworld (and psychologically viewed as the deep, dark interior world of the subconscious and dreams) gives the free soul the name "water soul", making its character distinctive to the windy breath soul.

Merkur writes:

"The free soul, which can leave and return to the body in sleep, trances, and illnesses without causing loss of life, is a genuinely distinct type of soul. Either it is (conceived of) as miniature and located in the body, or it follows the body as though it were a shadow. It has and imparts the shape and personality of the person or creature, according to the respective species and, at least in humans, *individuality*. It is the seat of all illness, for its loss (or injury) causes illness (to manifest in the body.) It is also the site of spirit-intrusion. Through illness, the free soul can be an indirect cause of death. However, shamans may journey safely out of their bodies as free souls during their so-called spirit flights.

At death, the free soul becomes the ghost. Either it journeys to an afterlife realm and in most cases (in most traditional Inuit thought) is reincarnated, or, because death taboos have been violated (or it died under other disturbing conditions), it remains earthbound and seeks vengeance. Violations of hunting taboos have similar effects on the free souls of animals."

The Free Soul remains connected to- in relationship to- the body and breath-soul, during a human life. During that life, all of these "three parts" work in some kind of accord. During a soul flight-type trance, or during any of the other times at which the free soul may be separate from the body and breath, it (the free soul) remains in communication, somehow with the breath and body; it remains in relationship, but it no longer acts in simple concert or in unison with them.

For the free soul to stray so far from the body and breath that it cannot return for some reason, or for it to become preyed upon by a spirit or another similar entity, to the point that it lacks the power to maintain the connection, will result in the death of a person. When we are conscious and awake, the free soul is, in a sense, "deactivated", and we are aware of the world through our breath and the mind that the breath-soul supports.

When we sleep, and have dreams (particularly deep, meaningful, or lucid dreams) or when we enter into trances for any reason (via intentional mystical efforts, intoxication, etc.) or when we are put into crisis by illness, injury, or some kind of ordeal, the free soul can become "active" and we may have visions or "out of body-type" experiences, or mystical experiences otherwise. When the breath soul is paralyzed by sleep or trance or changed conditions in the body, then the free soul seems able to become active, and our awareness becomes more centered within it.

There is some support for the idea that at death, the breath soul and free soul remain in communication and unison for a short while, before the breath soul is finally depersonalized or vanished. After that point, with the breath soul faded and the body returned to the elements of the world, the free soul alone journeys to whatever afterlife or dreams may come. It came from the depths, and recovers its home journeying back to those depths. It may be disempowered in life (or at any time) by being preyed upon by spirits or such beings; it can be lost, or lose or gain in power, but the Free Soul does not appear to be able to die; it is not mortal in the way the body and breath soul appear to be.

I make it a point to not discuss too much (speculate too much) on what the ever-journeying free soul is "doing." People wonder about whether it rejoins the breathing, sensual world over and over again, spending some periods of time in the Underworld and other periods in this world of life "up here above", going back and forth for some reason. I say "maybe." Or "If the free souls feel compelled to" or "If they choose to." I don't know that anyone can really say.

The going "back and forth" of the soul would be a kind of rebirth narrative. I think it possible, of course, and I incline to this belief, but as to the goals or motivations of the strange soul (for the free soul belongs to a world beyond the breath and its rational analysis) little can or perhaps should be said.

The free soul belongs to the truly mystical "side" of things, the dreaming of this world, the depths, the mysterious layers. What we need to learn about it is best learned relating to it, through trance, through sought-after experiences of a mystical variety, about which little can be said.

I will state, however, that in the free soul, in the wandering, journeying soul, I sense the undying aspect of every life. The breath soul has no real ability to comprehend this; from its perspective, death is a fade to black and nothingness. The breath soul and free soul come from two different worlds, though they relate and share together in many ways in this life. And yet, in ways, they remain strangers to one another.

We have a very hard time comprehending or understanding the surreal impact of our dreams, for upon awakening, as the breath-souled mind reasserts itself, the memories of the surreal deeper world and its dream-symbols are either dis-carded rapidly, or become objects of intellectual scrutiny, often to be discarded as "crazy" or "irrational" things. The country of dreams is close to the native country of the Free Soul, if it is not outright the same country.

Even if we could restore a person to life- restore the free soul to the body along with the breath soul, the person would likely either have no memory of anything, or not be able to make sense of what just happened. They would likely not be able to communicate what they just encountered, in any way that would make sense to living, breathing people.

4. Anthropological Rationale for the Two Souls Model

Merkur writes:

"In the view of Arbman, endorsed by Hultkrantz, soul dualism is "based upon entirely different psychic experiences." The breath-soul is based on the experience of conscious bodily life, and the free-soul on the experience during dreams and visions of self in a non-corporeal form. That the theory is correct there can be no serious question. The concept of the breath-soul serves to explain the difference between the living body and the corpse.

The concept of a second soul, a free soul, serves to explain how the self can become disembodied in trances, dreams, etc., even though the breath soul remains in the body and continues to imbue it with life. I would emphasize, however, the considerable difference between psychological experiences and elaborated ideas of souls."

World Indweller: The Cross of Life
Breath from the Sky, Dreams from the Deep

5. Phenomenological Insights Regarding the Soul and the Intersubjective World

We encounter life as a field of experience, a collective landscape; it is constituted of many experiencing subjects, as well as ourselves. But there are many things we experience that are *not* commonly shared.

Abram writes:

"When daydreaming, for example, my attention is carried by phenomena whose contours and movements I am able to alter at will, a whole phantasmagoria of images that nevertheless lack the solidity of bodies. Such forms offer very little resistance to my gaze. They are not, that is, held in places by *gazes other than my own*- these are entirely "my" images, "my" fantasies, "my" fears, "my" dreamings. And so I am brought, like Husserl, to recognize at least two regions of the experiential or phenomenal field: one of phenomena that unfold entirely for me- images that arise, as it were, on this side of my body- and another region of phenomena that are, evidently, responded to *and* experienced by other embodied subjects as well as by myself."

These latter phenomena are still subjective- they appear to me within a field of experience colored by my mood and my current concerns- and yet I cannot alter or dissipate them at will, for they seem buttressed by many involvements besides my own. That tree bending in the wind, this cliff wall, the cloud drifting overhead- these are not merely subjective; they are *intersubjective phenomenon*: phenomenon experienced by a multiplicity of sensing subjects."

This is a description of the "intersubjective field." It is a very potent re-framing of the standard dichotomy between "objective and subjective." Abram continues: "For the conventional contrast between the "subjective" and "objective" realities can now be reframed as a contrast *within the subjective field of experience itself*- as the felt contrast between subjective and intersubjective phenomena."

In other words, what we experience as "outside of us" are things that more than one person or sensing subject can sense or interact with. The things we experience as "inside us" are the things that appear to only be sensed by us. But there is only subjectivity and intersubjectivity- The pure "objectivity" assumed to exist by most modern science is nothing more than an *idealization of intersubjective experience*. It is another kind of culturally-constructed illusion. There is no way to rise "above" intersubjectivity; there is no way to be "outside of it"- because that would be a realm that could not exist.

This whole life-world, this Nature, this *reality* as we call it, is completely dependent on sensing subjects. These sensing expressions of its very vitality might be thought its basic building blocks, if it had building blocks: its basic constituents.

Things are "real" because they are sensed. And not just by us, but by countless things that sense. The oak tree we encounter on a visit to a park was there before our eyes sensed it, but before our eyes sensed it, a bird was walking on its branches, sensing it; the sun was shining down on it, and water inside it was moving through it. The tree itself was sensing those things. And that oak tree, like the birds on its branches- sensed you when you came by, each in their own unique ways.

The recursive nature of sensing- that you sense things and they sense you back- creates the communicative sensing river of intersubjectivity. The solidity of this world is found in precisely how we continually encounter others in it- and how they encounter us. There is no danger that the oak tree will vanish when I stop sensing it, nor is there any danger that it didn't exist before I did sense it- it was always the subject of the sensing of other beings, just as it made other beings and phenomena subjects of its own sensing.

And our bodies, being the objects of the sensing of countless other things, just as they in turn make the bodies of other things the object of their sensing, are important features in the midst of all this- without our bodies, we would not have any power to participate in the intersubjective field. In other words, we wouldn't exist as objects of the experience of anything; we would not be able to have another thing exist as an object of our experience.

None of the wise will downplay the importance of the body. We want to; our culture gives us countless reasons to; even the reduction of body to "mere elements", and the concomitant focus on "soul as immortal and beyond the body" is a dangerous divergence if we lack certain understandings.

The body is the soul's most tangible way of being present in the intersubjective field that we call "cosmos." During life, while the body, breath soul, and free soul (all of them being necessary mental abstractions, in a way) are together, relating so intimately and acting in unison, it is not unfair to say that the body *is* the soul; it is the chief means by which the soul interacts with other beings. The body might be thought of as the *soul intensified*.

Abram writes:

"The body is... a singularly important structure within the phenomenal field. The body is that mysterious and multifaceted phenomenon that seems always to accompany one's awareness within the field of appearances. Yet the phenomenal field also contains many other bodies- other forms that move and gesture in a fashion similar to one's own. While one's own body is experienced, as it were, only from within, these other bodies are experienced from outside; one can vary one's distance from these bodies and can move around them, while this is impossible in relation to one's own body... At the heart of your deepest, most abstract notions of "self" is the sensuousness and tangible reality of the body. At your depths, your emotions, feelings, dreams, thoughts, hopes, and body are all the same unified phenomenon."

The Intersubjective Field has more than just what we sense horizontally- it also has vertical *depths*, or a strange interior that is revealed in vision and dream. Those depths (or whatever variety of netherworldly form they become conceived into) can be associated with what mythology calls "The Underworld."

Death is the end of a personal horizontal experience of the intersubjective field, and an "expanding out", a journeying or sinking into the depths, into the massive and subtle field of more-than-human and other-than-human sensing perceptions and sensations. It's the free soul journeying, being the shape-shifter and the "deep diver", which it is. As Abram says, the soul after death *vitalizes the world in a new manner*.

We can conceive of the wandering soul intensifying itself, through unthinkable brilliance and with the alliance of many other powers, into this body we identify with and sense the entire world through.

And that body we call "physical" is also a shape-shifter, changing at every moment in response to will and to other forces and environment. The body's boundaries are not so simple as they have been made out; the body is almost holographic, totally enmeshed in the environment around us- completely honeycombed by countless other life-forms within it. It is totally responsive to the environment, and extremely biologically intelligent.

When we die, that wandering soul expands- moves- travels- flies- and then intensifies itself again- it takes on a new body or form in the *depths* of things. In a manner similar perhaps to how we "embody" ourselves in dreams when we fall asleep, the time of death is a transition for the wandering soul. It "re-bodies" itself in a new manner befitting the cur- rent conditions it experiences. And with that new body- another intensification of its presence as a being- it exists in another intersubjective manner, in another intersubjective community-field.

At the start of this short essay, I defined the soul as a living expression of the vitality of Nature itself. Now, I can state that while the breath soul and the free soul are both living expressions of the vitality of nature, that definition particularly refers, most centrally, to the free soul.

ABOUT THE AUTHOR

Robin Artisson lives in the *Green Meadow* of rural New England, sometimes on Maine's stony and forested shores, sometimes jaunting through the wooded interior, but always enjoying that region's four perfect seasons, its old and strange spirits, and its kindly and quiet people. He writes, conducts seminars devoted to spiritual ecology and sorcery, and is presently at work creating the *DeSavyok Elfhame Tarot* with artist Larry Phillips.

Printed in Great Britain
by Amazon